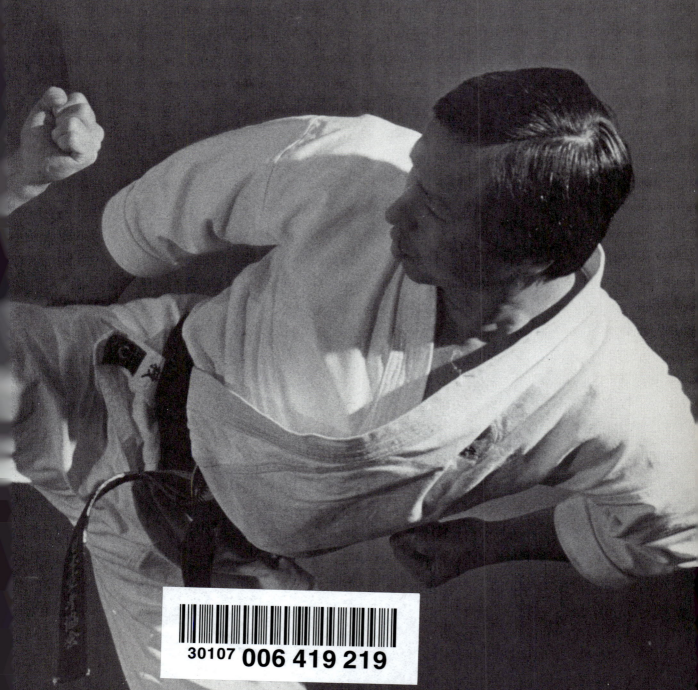

KNOW KARATE-DO

KNOW KARATE-DO

BRYN WILLIAMS

Photography: Robert Hope

William Luscombe Publisher Limited

First published in Great Britain by
William Luscombe Publisher Ltd
Artists House
14, Manette Street
London W1V 5LB
1975

IBSN 0 86002 039 8

Printed in Great Britain at the Alden Press, Oxford
and bound by Hunter & Foulis Ltd, Edinburgh

Contents

Forewords

To write a foreword to this book is both a duty and a pleasure. A duty because Bryn Williams, executive to the British Karate Control Commission and General Treasurer to the European Karate Union has, with a zest and generosity which have made him the admiration of the karateka of Europe, devoted part of his life and all his leisure time to the cause of our sport. The least I can do is to pay him this tribute.

A pleasure because Bryn Williams, although things have not always been easy between us, is a friend. We have had many bitter discussions, particularly at the beginning, when we did not fully understand each other. Even now that we understand each other better this is still so. This is the inevitable result of being pledged to an ideal like ours. Despite this there has developed a deep friendship which we cherish most carefully. A friendship which, through Bryn, has linked a generation of French and British *karateka*. This is more than a warmth of understanding; it has become a real brotherhood.

However, with my twenty years' karate experience, what surprises me most is that, through this book, I recognise the technical knowledge that Bryn Williams has acquired and which makes *Know Karate-do* such a well-researched book. It proves that the author is not only an executive of worth but an expert of the highest class.

I wish him every success both as an executive and as a writer. Equally I send my best wishes to the extraordinary British team which, by defeating Japan in the 1972 World Championships, became one of the legends of the Martial Arts.

J. Delcourt
Chairman, World Union of Karate-do Organisations
President, European Karate Union

British Karate owes much to Bryn Williams who has proved himself as a sportsman and administrator, winning the respect and affection of Karateka nationally.

Bryn Williams, an Economics Graduate who additionally was trained in Physical Education at Loughborough College, studied martial arts when working in the Far East. Combining his knowledge with driving zest and an eye for detail he has produced an authoritative book. *Know Karate-do* will be of interest to beginners and experts alike, for it examines and compares the major styles of Karate in addition to tracing the history and development of Karate as a whole.

It is significant how all whom he has consulted have readily and willingly helped with the technical and political detail: this I believe speaks for itself and confirms our high esteem and regard for the author.

Alan T. Francis, O.B.E.
Chairman, British Karate Control Commission

I am very grateful to Mr. B. Williams, Secretary, British Karate Control Commission, for his dedicating this book to all Karate-do enthusiasts.

I have had the opportunity of meeting Mr. Williams on several occasions and I am impressed by his long experience and enthusiasm and I think highly of his achievements in enhancing and diffusing the spirit of Karate.

I sincerely wish that this book will contribute to the correct understanding of Karate as an art which can be loved and enjoyed freely by all.

Eiichi Eriguchi
Chairman, Federation of All Japan Karate-do Organisations
General Secretary, World Union of Karate-do Organisations

Acknowledgements

The author wishes to acknowledge the considerable assistance and advice given by the B.K.C.C.'s Technical Advisers in the preparation of this book. He is particularly appreciative of his wife Mary's talent and patience in preparing illustrations and in proof reading. He also wishes to thank Mr. J. Delcourt, Mr. A. T. Francis and Mr. E. Eriguchi for generously agreeing to write Forewords and Mr. Peter R. Jordan, Medical Officer of the B.K.C.C. for contributing a chapter on 'Karate Injuries'. Thanks are also due to Mr. A. T. Francis, Chairman of the B.K.C.C., for his general encouragement and to Mr. N. Kitamura, Mr. H. Tomida and Mr. B. Fitkin for posing for photographs along with Mr. Enoeda and Mr. Suzuki. He would also like to thank Miss Ann MacLachlan for typing scripts and the many others who have helped in ways both large and small. Finally, he would like to express his gratitude to Mr. Wong Lun of Hong Kong for first introducing him to the Oriental Martial Arts.

The Author

To Clinton,

With very best wishes.

Bryn

Technical Advisers:

Keinosuke Enoeda
7th Dan (*Shotokan*)

Tatsuo Suzuki
7th Dan (*Wadoryu*)

Mitsusuke Harada
(*Shotokai*)

Steve Arneil
6th Dan (*Kyokushinkai*)

Steve Morris
6th Dan (*Gojuryu*)

Roy Stanhope
4th Dan (*Shukokai*)

1 The Origins of Karate and Related Arts

Karate as now practised is a product of 20th-century Japan, but its roots can be traced back via Okinawa and China—possibly to India of the 5th and 6th century BC. There are even those who claim a European influence stemming from the *pankration* techniques of ancient Greece. *Pankration* was a ferocious combination of wrestling and boxing not restrained by rules. The entire body was used as a weapon and contests frequently ended in death. Although abandoned by the Greeks it was re-introduced by the Romans to become a standard part of the gladiatorial programme. Although it cannot be proved with any certainty it is possible that some of those techniques had earlier been carried to India by the invading army of Alexander the Great in 336–323 BC. Even if this is true, however, it seems most unlikely that they had any long-term influence upon the development of Karate. *Europe*

India's contribution to Karate is much more probable although still not absolutely provable. Yoga originated in the Indus Valley many centuries BC and through the strong diaphragmatic breathing techniques involved may have had a substantial influence upon the combat systems of the Orient, including Karate. This influence would have taken two main forms. In the first place *karateka* (exponents of Karate) place special emphasis upon strong breathing to assist muscle contraction. The effect of this is to increase striking power. There is also a well-known relationship between the emotions and respiration and anyone who has been subject to fear or excitement will be aware that his breathing rate increased. Yogi exploit and reverse this relationship and by breath control induce a calming effect upon the emotions. *Karateka* also borrow this technique to ensure a state of mental calm. Special breathing techniques would therefore seem to be India's contribution to the development of Karate, although there is no conclusive proof of this. Some suggest that these breathing techniques were already built into Chinese Dowism and were not therefore an Indian import. Certain combat techniques involving joint *India*

Indian Temple Guardian

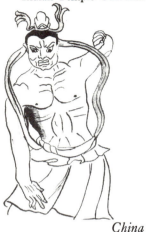

locks, strikes and throws were also categorised and recorded in the *Lotus Sutra* although these are not extensively used in Karate.

A fact that surprises many western observers is the relationship of Buddhist monks to Karate, particularly in its formative years. To those who think of monks in Christian terms such a relationship seems unnatural. However, the survival of wandering monks in both early India and China might well have rested on their ability to defend themselves. With the later development of Zen Buddhism, which stresses an acceptance of life as it is, a willingness and ability to live and die within the existing pattern, violently if necessary, also became, as it were, a doctrinal requirement. It was via such an Indian monk that the above breathing and, less probably, the fighting techniques are reputed to have been carried to China.

China

It is believed that in the 5th Century AD this Buddhist monk Bhodidharma (Daruma Taisha in Japanese) travelled from India to China eventually to teach at the monastery of *Shaolinssu* (*Shorin-ji* in Japanese) in Hunan province. To this half legendary figure is attributed the creation of both Zen Buddhism and a system of physical training which, by blending ingredients from Yoga and Indian and indigenous Chinese fighting techniques, was to lead to the foundation of the *Shaolinssu* temple system of fighting. This system was eventually to become famous throughout China. The supposed reason for this development is that in teaching his students the way of Zen he found that many were incapable of withstanding the severe physical as well as mental discipline involved. A form of physical training was therefore required and he evolved three training sequences or routines. At a much later date these were adapted into five sequences supposedly based on the movements of the dragon, the tiger, the leopard, the snake and the stork. As Chinese tradition, however, always demands a story to explain the origin of customs it is conceivable that the five descriptions are little more than an invention to meet that requirement. The five animal names could merely be pictorial images to describe five routines which respectively stress speed, total body movement, agility, fluidity and calmness. When in the 'cat stance' for example one certainly does not look like a cat, but one is well positioned to make the quick movements characteristic of that animal. The different Karate styles now emphasise these different qualities of movement to varying degrees.

The existence of this descriptive custom may also lead one to doubt the significance or even the existence of Bhodidharma as an individual, although most Chinese and Japanese historians appear to believe that he did exist. There are, however, several assessments as to his influence upon Zen and the fighting techniques of *Shaolinssu*. The question of his influence on Zen and the latter's effect upon Karate is discussed in Chapter 2. The fighting techniques attributed to him are, however, all practised in a static position, so it seems more than likely that they were devised as a system of exercise and breath control rather than as a method of combat. There is no doubt, however, that *Shaolinssu* did exist, that it was burnt down on two separate occasions and that it developed a famous school of fighting monks who were to influence the whole of Chinese *Kenpo* (fighting).

Shaolinssu boxing

The ancient Chinese also possessed substantial medical knowledge which they developed along lines quite different from those currently practised in the West. The increasing western respect for acupuncture is one indication of this skill. *Kenpo*, or *Kung Fu* as it is currently called, benefits from this knowledge in that the numerous vital spots on the human body to which the Chinese apply their medicines and acupuncture techniques became the target for *Kenpo* and subsequently for Karate attacks.

Although the influence of *Shaolinssu* gradually spread throughout China, it naturally developed different forms according to local conditions. South China for example is a land of paddy fields and boatmen where bending and pulling is part of everyday life. This builds strong upper bodies at the expense of the legs. Southern styles therefore tend to emphasise arm and head movements. Many of the hand movements are also of an open hand or clawing and gripping nature. Kicks above groin height are rare. In contrast, the men of the north tend to be horsemen. This leads to the development of strong legs and consequently to a greater emphasis upon jumping, kicking and rolling. These latter techniques are also similar to *Tae-Kwon-do* which evolved in neighbouring Korea.

Compared with the Japanese-based styles, relatively little is known in the West of the Chinese styles, apart from *Tai Chi Chuan* (Supreme Ultimate Fist) and *Kung Fu*. *Kung Fu* like Karate is an all-embracing term currently used to indicate martial arts indigenous to China as opposed to Japan. As with Karate, there are a variety of styles some of which are hard and others soft. As the Chinese away from home are undoubtedly insular, tending to live in their own communities and passing their skills on only to relatives and friends, very little is known of the many styles that exist. With access to China in the 1970s becoming relatively easier and the consequent wave of *Kung Fu* films that has swept the West, interest in and probably knowledge of the Chinese martial arts is likely to increase considerably during the coming years.

The basic difference between the Karate and *Kung Fu* lies in the latter's use of clawing and gripping hand movements. Many of these have been or are being eliminated from those Karate styles which particularly emphasise competition, as clawing, gouging, kneeing, butting and ripping are obviously not permissible. *Kung Fu* blocks to fist attacks tend to be with the open hand, leading to the application of locks, throws and gripping attacks to nerve centres. At the present time it is purely a form of combat or self defence and has no rules which enable any aspect of it to be considered as a competitive sport. In this respect it is perhaps psychologically and technically more akin to *Jui Jitsu* than most styles of Karate. *Kung Fu* foot attacks above groin height are also rarer than in Karate, although there are numerous attacks to the ankle, knee and groin. The Chinese, especially those of the south, believe that high leg attacks create dangerous imbalance and vulnerability. Some *Kung Fu* films do include extensive use of high kicks but this can be misleading. Many of these films were made employing as many, if not more, Karate as *Kung Fu* experts and presumably these techniques were retained not only because of their spectacular nature but because of the actors' prior experience. These films were after all made for entertainment not documentary or educative purposes and should be accepted as such. The discipline and atmosphere within a Karate class also tends to be much more formal than *Kung Fu*, possibly due to the more militaristic traditions of the Japanese. To a Japanese the idea of wearing shoes or smoking in the *dojo* would be heretical—to a more easy-going Chinese, who also normally teaches smaller select groups, such informality would be normal.

Tai Chi Chuan (Supreme Ultimate Fist) or *Tai Chi* as it is more commonly known is more a formalised sequence of exercises than a system of combat. It is performed slowly and with graceful continuity. It has both long and short variations, the former containing 108 positions each of which are named and follow in sequence. The individual movements have intriguing names such as 'the white crane spreads its wings', 'returning to the mountain carrying a tiger' and 'catching the peacock's tail', etc. The movements all depend on circular motion and there is always a withdrawal before an advance. The principle is to retire before an opponent's attack and to counter attack only when he has over-reached himself. This principle also applies to some Karate styles.

In the parks of Hong Kong one can frequently see groups of Chinese, both old and young, practising the sequences together in graceful harmony. As a point of interest it is also said that the nationalist warriors of the Boxer rising practised *Tai Chi* before going into combat with the modern semi-colonial army of General Gordon in 1896. The rising was named after this custom.

Tai Chi

Okinawa

Between Japan and Taiwan (Formosa) the islands of the Ryukyu chain are dotted over the East China sea. The largest of these islands is Okinawa lying on the main commercial and military routes. It was therefore inevitably influenced by both China and Japan. Combat techniques known as *Te* (hand) had existed for many centuries in Okinawa but with the unification of the country in 1470 and the imposition of laws banning the carrying of arms, *Te* underwent considerable, although clandestine, development. Being unable to carry arms legally, the ability to defend oneself unarmed was obviously popularised. The object was definitely functional not sporting. Some Okinawan styles still tend to avoid the sport element in Karate and concentrate on *Kata*.

With a later occupation by the Satsuma clan, driven out of Japan following their defeat in a civil war in 1600, *Te* received a further boost. In contrast to the rounded Chinese forms, *Te* was mainly a hard, square form of combat. It also entailed substantial conditioning (building up of protective callouses) as it was necessary to break through the protective wooden armour of the occupiers with the bare hands and feet when striking at their vital parts. It is also probable that they used a form of 'knuckle-duster'. With the arrival of Chinese immigrants, and political refugees, a blending of the two forms evolved. This influence was accentuated by the activities of substantial fleets of highly organised Chinese pirates which on occasions virtually controlled the China seas.

In recognition of this Chinese influence *Te* became known as *Tang hand*, *Tang* being the name of a Chinese dynasty the symbol of which became associated with China in general. Okinawa still recognises this considerable Chinese influence. Possibly due to their own martial traditions, Japan does not recognise quite the same degree of mainland influence. *Tang hand* however is the basis of contemporary Karate which was carried to Japan in the early 20th century. The significance of Okinawa can also be seen at modern Karate tournaments when demonstrations are almost invariably given in the fighting usages to which Okinawan agricultural implements were deceptively put. These implements include the *Tonfa* (a form of halter worn around the neck of cattle), the *Tsai* (an agricultural fork with the two outside prongs sawn off) and the *Nunchaku* (a universally hinged flail). These usages evolved, as did *Tang hand*, out of the ban on the possession of arms.

Japan   Meanwhile feudal Japan had its own fighting traditions and *Jui Jitsu* was as much a weapon of the *Samurai* as was the sword. *Jui Jitsu* incorporated a whole range of fighting techniques but with the abolition of the *Samurai* in 1867 it withered away as a lethal form of combat unsuited to a modern society. Certain elements, however, were retained and emerged as *Aikido* and the modern sport of *Judo*, both of which use the principle of exploiting opponent's movements rather than dynamically blocking them as in some Karate techniques. Swordsmanship became *Kendo*, a form of fencing using wooden or bamboo instead of steel swords

Kyudo

Kendo

and *Kyudo*, a kind of archery, maintained another of the *Samurai* traditions.

Sumo wrestling, an ancient form of combat peculiar to Japan now involves giants often of 20 stone or more. Originally, these were chosen fighters representing different groups, called in to settle disputes in tournament manner. Contests originally included kicking, butting, striking, etc., with the aim basically being to down the opponent and trample him into submission. Such tournaments later took on a religious significance comparable to that of the Ancient Olympic Games. During the Tokugawa era (1600–1867), it became fashionable for Lords to patronise wrestlers. In 1909, with modifications to the rules, it became a professional sport with a large spectator following. There are now six major tournaments a year, each of which run for fifteen days. The martial arts of the *Samurai* therefore survived, albeit in a modified form.

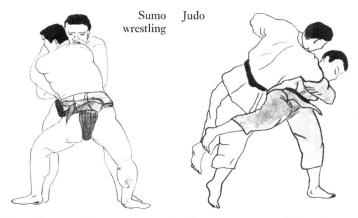

Sumo
wrestling   Judo

One element, however, remained as a common denominator. The word *do* in *Karate-do*, *Judo* and *Kendo* means 'way'. In other words these sports or arts are regarded as a way of life contributing to the character building of the *Samurai* type. Technical training is supplemented by the cultivation of 'fighting spirit'. In fact some consider the psychological and moral attributes of the athlete to be more significant than the physical and technical. This 'spiritual' attitude derives from the philosophy of the *Samurai* for whom combat was a matter of life or death not merely a recreation. It can be developed by the voluntary acceptance of pain and the determination not to give in. Even a man with a broken arm might still win if he fights on. In the past, this fighting spirit could be developed in genuine fighting situations. For the *Samurai* there was after all no referee to call a halt. Nowadays such spirit can only be developed by a form of self-generated torture.

The first Okinawan to take *Tang hand* to Japan was Funakoshi Gichin who gave his first demonstration in 1917. He was also fond of poetry and adopted the pen name 'Shoto' from a Chinese poem that he liked. In the early years he used *Judo* and *Kendo dojos* for practice but when his own permanent *dojo* was opened in 1936 it was called the *Shotokan*, meaning Shoto's house or hall. This was later to become the name of a style. In 1936 the name *Tang* was also dropped and certain elements of Japanese *Jui-jitsu* and other martial arts having been incorporated the Japanese word *Karate* (empty hand) was substituted. Some Japanese would also claim that they brought to the art a 'fighting spirit' formerly lacking. Doubtless many Okinawans and Chinese would dispute this.

The new name, however, was chosen for reasons one of which is as subtle as the other is obvious. The purely physical significance of 'empty hand' needs no explanation. However, 'emptiness' has considerable significance in Zen Buddhism and as Funakoshi stated:

'As a mirror's polished surface reflects whatever stands before it and a quiet valley carries even small sounds, so must the student of Karate render his mind empty of selfishness and wickedness in an effort to react appropriately towards anything he might encounter. This is the meaning of "Kara" or empty in Karate.'

To a sceptical westerner such a statement is apt to sound pretentious if not absurd. At best it appears to be an attempt to give a fighting technique a moral conscience and respectability. It is hoped that Chapter 2 will help remove such scepticism. Funakoshi's statement is also in line with the Chinese concept of *mushin no shin* (mind of no mind) in which one is totally immune to outsiders. It implies a receptive, pliant and spontaneous mind reacting instinctively to situations as they occur, even to the point of acquiring a sixth sense. It certainly does not involve a state of mental and psychological coma, as the phrase probably suggests to most westerners.

In the years following Funakoshi's arrival several other styles developed, some being introduced by other Okinawan masters. Each used its own techniques, *Katas* and training methods which were jealously guarded. Rivalry between these groups was intense and the proliferation of styles meant that Karate was exceptionally fragmented.

Okinawan Styles:
Uechiryu
Ishinryu
Shorinjeryu
Shoreijiryu. Founder: Higanuma
Gojuryu. Founder: Chojun Miyagi

Japanese originated styles include:
Shotokan. Founder: Funakoshi Gichin (born 1870, Okinawa)
Wadoryu. Founder: Hironori Otsuka (born Japan)
Shukokai. Founder: Chojiro Tani (born Japan)
Kyokushinkai. Founder: Masutatsu Oyama (born 1923, Korea)
Shitoryu. Founder: Kenwa Mabuni (born Okinawa)

During the war it is understood that all the *Budo* arts were controlled by the *Budokukai,* a Government Department concerned with defence. As Karate was considered an Okinawan rather than an indigenous Japanese art, it was not permitted to join except via the Judo section. This it did not do. At the end of the war all the *Budo* arts were banned by the occupying forces, although doubtless they continued to be practised secretly. In 1947, however, as Karate had not been linked to the *Budokukai,* it is believed that General MacArthur, on the request of a Professor from Waseda University, permitted Karate clubs to be re-opened. Similar permission was not granted to other *Budo* organisations until later.

The next year the Japanese Karate Association was formed. It originally aimed at being an all-style organisation but, when several major styles refused to join, it confined itself to the *Shoto* group of which Funakoshi was head. By the mid 1950s, with Funakoshi now aged ninety, differences began to emerge within the group concerning future policy. The JKA were rapidly developing into a highly organised, modern association of professional instructors with economic as well as technical objectives. They were also beginning to expand overseas. Some members, including five Universities, opposed this tendency and broke away in 1956 to retain an amateur approach. The modern JKA became known as practitioners of *Shotokan* Karate and the amateur splinter as *Shotokai.* The JKA is now possibly the largest single organisation of professional instructors in the world whilst *Shotokai* has gradually diminished and has no effective Japanese or World organisation. The latter survives in Britain and Europe through the instruction of M. Harada, who himself studied under Funakoshi. Although preferring the amateur approach, he became professional almost by accident, and helps perpetuate the *Shotokai* group.

Although techniques have diverged somewhat over the years, *Shotokai karateka* do not consider their technique to be basically different from *Shotokan.* They also believe that Karate is Karate and that none of the styles' differences are fundamental and that the proliferation of styles is the product more of economics and Karate politics than technique.

World expansion Since the late 1950s the spread of Karate from Japan overseas has been quite phenomenal. In Britain at that time there was barely a handful of *karateka*. By 1974 there were at least 50,000 and the growth rate continues. A similar pattern is reflected in many other countries.

In a further attempt to unify Karate, the various Japanese associations in 1964, at the time of the Olympic Games, formed the Federation of All Japan Karatedo Organisations (FAJKO) and drew up a set of rules which could be used for competition of an inter-style nature. The first World Championships were held in Tokyo and Osaka in 1970. Thirty-two nations were represented and at the accompanying Conference the World Union of Karate-do Organisations (WUKO) was formed. Karate had truly arrived as a world sport. Japan won both the team and individual championships. What happened in the second World Championships in Paris in 1972 was to cause a sensation and is described in Chapter 10.

2 The Influence of Feudal Japan and Samurai Attitudes upon Karate

'Those who cling to life die,
Those who defy death live.'
                    Uyesugi Kenshin
                    (16th century)

Although modern Karate is a 20th-century development, derived from Okinawa, it is now strongly influenced by the psychology of the Japanese martial arts with their associated feudal origins and attitudes. It is therefore difficult if not impossible to understand it fully without knowing something of that culture. The purpose of this chapter is to describe that culture in so far as it is relevant to a study of Karate.

With the forcible opening of Japan by American naval power to western trade in 1853 and the consequent end of feudalism, the *Samurai* or warrior class, which numbered nearly 2,000,000 out of a total population of approximately 30,000,000, became an anachronism and, notwithstanding several revolts, were pensioned off. Despite their demise as a social class, however, the whole of Japanese culture, art and literature was steeped to the core with the traditions of the *Samurai* and this spirit still survives and manifests itself in a variety of ways. Not the least of these is in the martial arts including Karate, as well as in the psychology that motivated the *Kamikaze* or suicide pilots of the second World War, the jungle survival and continued resistance for 29 years following the war of ultra-nationalist Japanese soldiers such as Lieutenant Onoda in the Philippines, and in Japan's post war aggressive economic policies. Many Japanese still look back to the feudal period as a heroic and romantic age in which the *Samurai* was the hero figure.

'As among flowers the cherry is queen, so among men the *Samurai* is Lord,' go the words of a Japanese song.

In order to understand Karate it is therefore necessary to appreciate the spirit of the *Samurai* which still motivates many of the world's top *karateka*. This of course is not to imply that such a spirit motivates most western, or for that matter all Japanese *karateka*. Many of the former in particular treat it purely as a method of combat or self defence and are only dimly aware of what might be called the underlying philosophy. It is hoped that this book will help to bridge that gap.

The Japanese feudal period lasted from the late 12th to the mid-19th century and is in many respects comparable to its European counterpart. Both possessed rigid, hierarchical class structures and a strict code of ethics for the warrior class. In Japan this code was known as *Bushido* which literally translated means 'Military, Knight, Ways' or the code of conduct appropriate to a fighting Knight. At the apex of the social pyramid was

Three classes:
Samurai, Merchant
and Peasant

the Emperor or 'Son of Heaven' who until 1945 was worshipped as a living god, but who for most of the feudal period had no practical involvement in the affairs of state. His main function lay in fostering the culture and self-conscious artistry of the courtly life, architecture, landscape gardening, poetry and geisha girls to each of which rigid rules applied. Political power lay in the hands of the *Shogun* or 'General' who personified the Storm God or spiritual father of the *Samurai*. His powers combined those of a contemporary Prime Minister and military leader. Beneath the

Shogun came the *daimyo* or court nobles, each of whom possessed a retinue of attendants or guards (*Bushi* or *Samurai*) which amounted to a small private army. The remaining social classes in descending order of importance but not necessarily wealth were the peasantry, the artisans and the merchants. It is interesting to note that the relatively wealthy merchants were the social inferiors of the peasants and the artisans as well as of the *Samurai*. The *Samurai* were debarred from commerce and received their payment in the form of rice from the *Shogun* or *daimyo* which in later years, with the development of money as a medium of exchange, they generally sold to the merchants. Many lived in a state of defiant poverty considering it bad taste to talk about or be overconcerned with money. Despite this they became the ideal of the nation and a, if not the, major subject of art and literature.

What were the influences which went to mould the *Samurai*? These were undoubtedly Zen Buddhism, Shinto and the teachings of Confucius.

'Meeting a Zen master on the road
Face him with neither words nor silence   *Zen*
Give him an uppercut
And you will be called one who understands Zen'[1]

[1] *Zen Flesh*, *Zen Bones*, Penguin Books, p. 122.

Zen is one of the many branches of Buddhism practised in Japan. It originated in China. Some believe that it was devised by the half-legendary Bodhidharma to meet the practical rather than the contemplative needs of the pragmatic Chinese. Others consider that it was the product of a whole school of teachers and possibly resulted from a blending of the more intellectual Mahayana Buddhism and indigenous Chinese Taoism.

It is neither a religion nor a philosophy in the normal sense but—as described by Dr. C. G. Jung, the eminent Swiss psychologist, in his foreword to D. T. Suzuki's book, *An Introduction to Zen Buddhism*—more a technique of psycho-analysis leading to enlightenment. Not believing in original sin, devotees believe that in all things there exists part of the Buddha nature. To recognise this Buddha nature is to identify with it and to achieve enlightenment or *Satori*.

'The Buddha himself
Was once a man like us
We too at the end
Shall become Buddha

All creatures may share the nature of Buddha
How grievous indeed
That this is not known!'

by Hecke Monogatari
(Heian period 794–1184 AD)[2]

[2] *The Penguin Book of Japanese Verse*, translated by Geoffrey Bownas and Anthony Thwaite, 1964.

The first step towards enlightenment is therefore to understand oneself—not merely an unreal, possibly romanticised image of oneself.

'This body is the *Bodhi*-tree (True Wisdom)
The mind is like a mirror bright;
Take heed to keep it always clean
And let not dust collect upon it'[3]

[3] From *The Zen Doctrine of No Mind* by D. T. Suzuki (Publisher: Rider and Co.).

Zen is therefore individualistic and there is no moral stress on good or bad but merely understanding reality, which inevitably contains good and bad as it does black and white or up and down. Buddha himself is almost totally ignored. With this emphasis upon reality, Zen is not institutionally organised into a church system and the world, nature and life constitute reality. In this respect it is admirably suited to the world-orientated and practical natures of the Japanese. As the world can also be violent, an understanding of Zen involves an appreciation of this fact: hence the quotation at the beginning of this section. Seen in this context the association of Buddhist priests with the development of fighting techniques also becomes less of a mystery.

To understand oneself, however, involves delving into one's subconscious, as our conscious awareness reveals no more of our true nature than the tip of an iceberg reaching out of murky depths. For our subconscious to be made totally apparent in conscious form is obviously impossible as no one could comprehend such a potentially enormous number of ideas or images simultaneously without lapsing into confusion. To comprehend one's subconscious by an intellectual process is therefore impossible. Zen, however, aims to achieve this comprehension by an intuitive process. This involves the use of a technique (and the word 'Zen' can simply be translated as 'technique') designed to eliminate conscious awareness or thought which thus permits a sinking into one's subconscious where 'thy own original features which thou hadst before coming into existence'[4] can be ap-

[4] D. T. Suzuki, *Introduction to Zen Buddhism* (Publisher: Rider and Co.), p. 21.

preciated. The nearest thing to which a westerner might compare it is the achievement of a religious revelation or understanding by means other than prayer or the contemplation of holy relics. The standard means of achieving this is by intellectually 'letting oneself go' and by contemplating a *Koan* or paradox to which there is no logical answer but to which intuitively there is one or possibly more than one answer. To attempt to define a *Koan* and the processes of contemplation and *Satori* (enlightenment) involved is certainly beyond the writer's ambitions or competence. However, the following anecdote, often used as a *Koan* and which is extracted from Eugen Herrigel's book, *The Method of Zen*, is quoted to help explain what is meant.

'One day as Hyakujo stepped out of the house with his Master, Baso, they saw a flight of wild geese. Baso asked: "Where are they flying?" "They have already flown away, Master." Suddenly Baso seized Hyakujo by the nose and twisted it. Overcome by pain, Hyakujo cried out "O, oh!"

"You say they have flown away", said Baso, "but they have all been here from the beginning."

Then Hyakujo's back ran with sweat, and he had *satori*.

The difference between these two statements is so enormous that they cannot be reconciled with one another. "They have flown away" is a self evident statement of ordinary common sense. They are no longer visible, they have disappeared somewhere, hence they are no longer here and are not present for me. No illumination is needed to establish that fact.

Baso sees quite differently.

Seeing with your natural eyes, which everyone possesses from birth, can only mean registering what comes before your eyes at any moment, out of all that exists. In order for something to come before your eyes, it must exist. With the "third" eye, which is acquired only when one is "reborn", you see just this existence of something that is, the ground of its being. Therefore the statement must be: "They have always been here"—naturally not at this point of space, as space and time have no part in this vision. What is bound to appear senseless, perverse, a poor joke, is thus in reality a quite simple statement of fact—a fact which Baso sees as clearly and as corporeally as Hyakujo sees the fact that the geese have flown away. Neither of these facts refutes the other, as they belong to totally different dimensions, and Hyakujo would never have been able to find the solution by prolonged reflection. Only at the moment of acute pain which stopped him from thinking, did he find the solution through *satori*.'[5]

[5] *Method of Zen* by Eugen Herrigel (Publisher: Routledge & Kegan Paul), pp. 33–4.

Something of the same idea is implicit in the Christian doctrine which asks 'Has God any beginning?', and replies, 'He has no beginning. He always was. He is and always will be.'

Traditionally recognising a strong connection between the physical and the spiritual aspects of life, the Japanese accepted Zen from China in the 12th century and nourished it to full fruition. Although Zen did not actively encourage violence, it passively sustained it, due to its indifferent attitude to life and death. The *Samurai* class were particularly attracted by the concepts of loyalty, indifference to physical hardship and single-mindedness, which Zen engendered and the stoic beliefs in a trust in fate, submission to the inevitable and a disdain for life. The moral attitude of not looking back once committed to a course of action also appealed. Zen therefore became the creed of the warrior and subsequently the athlete classes. In a sense the *Samurai* already had Zen attitudes before they were aware of Zen. It is almost a question of whether Zen defines the *Samurai* or the *Samurai* defines Zen.

The contemplation of *Koans* is the standard Zen technique for achieving *satori*. There are, however, other techniques which whilst possibly not being substitutes can certainly be considered as complementary.

'The Great Path has no gates
Thousands of roads enter it,
When one passes through its gateless gate
He walks freely between earth and heaven.'[6]

[6] *Zen Flesh, Zen Bones*, Penguin Books, p. 94.

These alternative gates include the study of Japanese swordsmanship and archery, Karate, flower arranging (*ikebana*) and the tea ceremony. Each in its own way involves substantial self discipline, concentration, calmness of mind, composure and a quiet demeanour and each at its highest levels involves the application of techniques which become so instinctive that a conscious concentration upon detail is not required. The participant becomes aware of the sum total of his, or her, environment or in the case of

Karate the movement of the adversary without consciously thinking about the detailed movement of arms or legs, etc. In other
words he does not fail to see the wood for the trees. Opponents in
a contest therefore become not merely opposing forces but, like
life and death, part of one reality.

'Both the slayer
And the slain
Are like a dew-drop and a flash of lightning;
They are thus to be regarded.'
        (Attributed to a Japanese warrior as he died
                                beneath the sword)[7]

[7] *The Zen Doctrine of No Mind* by D. T. Suzuki (Publisher: Rider & Co.),
p. 119.

By moving as one unit in a total pattern of movement with the
adversary, with 'a mind like unruffled water' unaware of fear or
ego or other aspects of consciousness, one can, properly trained,
react immediately and appropriately to the opponent's movements. To watch expert *karateka*, especially when performing
Kata, is like watching someone in a trance. It is as if their consciousness were stripped away and they achieved a total identification with their skill. With a real master the same detachment can
be seen in combat. He appears unconcerned with his opponent's
movements or his own. He merely responds instinctively,
anticipating the opponent's vulnerability a fraction of a second
before it occurs. By the time that he is consciously aware of the
opportunity, the opportunity would have gone. Instinctiveness is
therefore the essence and this implies an absence of conscious
thought.

'All is emptiness—even the thought of emptiness is no longer
there. From this absolute emptiness comes the most wonderous
unfoldment of doing.'

Shinto

If Zen emphasised the military virtues of stoicism and disdain
for life and provided a technique for the training of instinctiveness, Shinto stressed loyalty to the Sovereign and patriotism. As
with Zen, Shinto stresses the basic goodness of the soul and the
infallibility of conscience. The interior of Shinto temples are also
very simple: there being no objects of worship other than a single
hanging mirror. The act of worship therefore becomes an appeal
to 'know thyself'. Obviously Zen and Shinto are naturally com-
patible in several respects and on occasions the two have been
institutionally related coming under the same government

department. It could be said that Shinto in particular fulfilled the role of an established church.

Shinto also involves an element of ancestor and nature worship and at the head of the national family stood the Emperor, the living embodiment of Japan. The land of Japan (*Nippon* or *Yamato*) was also the resting place of the Gods and dead ancestors and as such amounted to a holy land for which no sacrifice was too great. The suicide squads and *Kamikaze* pilots of the second World War, whilst possibly seeming a maniacal phenomena to the individualist orientated West, fall directly within the tradition of the *Samurai*.

'Full well I knew this course must end in death;
It was Yamato spirit urged me on
To dare whate'er betide'
      (Yoshida Shoin: on the eve of his execution)[8]

[8] *Bushido: The Soul of Japan*, Prof. Nitobe (Ohara Publications), p. 115.

With a state religion of this nature it is hardly surprising that the *Samurai*, or in modern times the Japanese army, should constitute a most formidable fighting force particularly in defence of their beloved homeland.

A mountain scene in Japan

'In the land of Yamato
The mountains cluster;
But the best of all mountains
Is Kagu, dropped from heaven.
I climbed, and stood, and viewed my lands.

Over the broad earth
Smoke-mist hovers.
Over the broad water
Seagulls hover.
Beautiful, my country,
My Yamato,
Island of the dragon fly.'
    (Emperor Jomei, 'Climbing Mount Kagu'—AD 593 to 641)[9]

[9] *Penguin Book of Japanese Verse.*

Undoubtedly it is the same group loyalty, pride and disciplined collective will that is the secret of Japan's current economic success.

Confucius

The third major formative influence upon the attitudes of *Samurai* were the teachings of Confucius, which treated government as a problem of ethics. Confucius was a Chinese philosopher who lived from 550–478 BC. He believed that all men were basically good and that all would be well with the world if the proper relationships were observed between superior and inferior. If a ruler acted properly so would his ministers and the general population would then accept their right to govern. Inferiors would retain their loyalty and respect for authority in return for which superiors would earn this respect by properly, benignly and with impartiality performing their duties. In some respects one could be describing the political ethics of *Tom Brown's School Days* or 19th-century Imperial Britain. This philosophy laid the basis for the *noblesse oblige* and benign paternalism of *Bushido*. Emphasising as it did the need for unity within a hierarchical society it was also naturally acceptable to the Shogunate as it constituted a further social cement.

The Codes of Zen, Shinto and Confucius therefore reinforced each other and provided a moral and philosophical basis for the attitudes of the *Samurai*.

Bushido : The Samurai Code

Attitudes towards the *Samurai* vary substantially. To some they were ferocious, professional fighters and ruthless killers. Romanticists see them as idealists comparable to the knights of Arthurian legends. Doubtless the truth lies somewhere between the extremes. They had many privileges, did not work and were exempt taxes. They also possessed the legal right to kill a disrespectful commoner on the spot. Some moral code was obviously required to prevent such powers being totally abused. Such a code, the *Bushido*, although unwritten, emerged in the 12th century.

Bushido means the code of conduct proper to a fighting knight. It is remarkably similar to that of the European Feudal Knights, whose historic period is also rather similar.[10] To live according to

[10] The Japanese feudal period lasted from the late 12th to the mid-19th century, whilst in Europe in general it is considered to have been from the 9th to the mid-16th century.

this code a *Samurai* would be brave, honourable, motivated by a desire to act with rectitude and justice, be merciful, truthful, polite, loyal, possess self control and be capable of self-sacrifice.[11]

[11] The European code of chivalry consisted primarily of: gallantry, honourableness, courtesy, idealism and an inclination to defend the weaker party.

A demanding code indeed, which doubtless more than a few failed to live up to. In the writer's experience, however, it is remarkable how many of these characteristics are still exhibited by many of the world's top *karateka*, especially those with a background of training in Japan. Presumably this is because they were trained in a setting steeped in these underlying traditions. A much larger proportion of Western *karateka* are trained in an atmosphere which emphasises the purely physical or even the commercial. Perhaps this is unavoidable as it is virtually impossible to transplant a whole cultural approach. This is especially so when the instruction is not in the hands of a Japanese, or of someone trained in Japan, or if language problems exist.

The *Bushido* emphasis upon the military virtue of bravery is inevitable and needs no enlargement. It is, however, closely linked to that of honour which is still a strong motivating force in Japan today. With the recent phenomenal economic rise of Japan, westerners are apt to think of that country as being primarily money motivated. This was not true of feudal Japan and if it is true today it is a motive superimposed upon that of honour. To the Japanese the forced opening up of their country to western trade in 1853 was a great humiliation and to restore face (honour) they needed to beat the West at its own game. Hence the social revolution, the abolition of the Shogunate and the *Samurai* which had failed to repel the barbarians and the emphasis upon economic and industrial as well as modern military strength. It was simply the *Bushido* spirit adapted to modern circumstances. Honour and self respect were the prime motives and wealth very much a secondary consideration although doubtless now it has become a symbol of success and therefore proof of the restoration of face. Among the world's top *karateka*, honour and fame is still a major driving force although the demand for Karate instructors being as great as it is, strong financial considerations inevitably apply. As the western feudal code of chivalry has long since been dead and

Samurai

buried, perhaps it is unreasonable to expect the Japanese to adhere to their *Bushido* principles for more than a century since the collapse of its basic *raison d'être*. If so, it is a great pity. Hopefully, these latter-day *Samurai* may continue to agree with their own *Samurai* forbears, for many of whom the loss of honour meant ritual *Seppuku* (*Hara-kiri*), that:

'When honour's lost, 'tis a relief to die;
Death's but a sure retreat from infamy.'

Let us hope, with Professor Nitobe that '*Bushido* as an independent code of ethics may vanish, but its power will not perish from the earth; its schools of martial prowess or civic honour may be demolished, but its fight and its glory will long survive their ruins.'[12]

[12] I. Nitobe, *Bushido : The Soul of Japan* (Ohara Publications).

Seppuku as such is unassociated with Karate although, in so far as its practice was observed by the *Samurai*, it has some vague psychological associations. It is certainly true that it fascinates many *Karateka* who look to Japan with a veneration which Muslims reserve for Mecca. For reasons of interest rather than relevance therefore the following section has been included.

For the *Samurai*, death involved a question of honour and death from old age and natural causes was not something to be desired. Like the ancient Greeks who believed that a noble, early and violent death was a sign of favour by the Gods, 'To live beautifully and to die beautifully' was his ideal. Hence the adoption of the cherry blossom as the emblem of the *Samurai*—beautiful and short lived. One day in full bloom, the next destroyed by the storm. 'To live happily ever after' was a totally alien concept and remains so in contemporary Japanese literature. Deliberately to seek out death, however, was a sign of cowardice and escapism. An admirable man would live his life as nobly as he could and only in certain prescribed circumstances could he resort to *Seppuku* or *Hara-kiri* (meaning literally 'belly-cut') as an honourable escape. These circumstances included avenging one's friends, making retribution for a crime or mistake, or avoiding disgrace. The most famous illustration of mass *Seppuku* concerns the 47 Ronin whose story is recorded in *Kabuki* plays and which amounts to the Japanese equivalent of a Greek tragedy.

The story goes as follows. In 1703 two *daimyo*, Lords Asano and Kira were present at the imperial court. An argument occurred in which Kira insulted Asano. Asano thereupon drew his sword and wounded Kira. It being a crime to draw a sword in the

Seppuku or Hara-kiri
(suicide by disembowelment)

imperial court, Asano was condemned to die by *Seppuku*, leaving his 47 *Samurai* without their Lord. They thereupon determined to avenge their master and entering Kira's mansion by night demanded that he, too, commit *Seppuku*. This being refused they cut off his head and placed it on Asano's grave. They then all committed *Seppuku* and were buried side by side. This act is revered in Japan as a manifestation of total loyalty and annual memorial services are held to commemorate it.

Seppuku was also institutionalised into a formal state means of execution which enabled the victim to retain honour through the death being self-imposed. A similar custom was also prevalent in ancient Rome. The following account of formal *Seppuku* is recorded in Mitford's (later Lord Redesdale's) *Tales of Old Japan*.

'We [seven foreign representatives] were invited to follow the Japanese witness into the *hondo* or main hall of the temple, where the ceremony was to be performed. It was an imposing scene. A large hall with a high roof supported by dark pillars of wood. From the ceiling hung a profusion of those huge gilt lamps and ornaments peculiar to Buddhist temples. In front of the high altar, where the floor, covered with beautiful white mats, is raised some three or four inches from the ground, was laid a rug of scarlet felt. Tall candles placed at regular intervals gave out a dim mysterious light, just sufficient to let all the proceedings be seen. The seven Japanese took their places on the left of the raised floor, the seven foreigners on the right. No other person was present.

After the interval of a few minutes of anxious suspense, Taki Zenzaburo, a stalwart man thirty-two years of age, with a noble air, walked into the hall attired in his dress of ceremony, with the peculiar hempen-cloth wings which are worn on great occasions. He was accompanied by a *kaishaku* and three officers, who wore the *jimbaori* or war surcoat with gold tissue facings. The word *kaishaku*, it should be observed, is one to which our word executioner is no equivalent term. The office is that of a gentleman; in many cases it is performed by a kinsman or friend of the condemned, and the relation between them is rather that of principal and second than that of victim and executioner. In this instance, the *kaishaku* was a pupil of Taki Zenzaburo, and was selected by friends of the latter from among their own number for his skill in swordsmanship.

With the *kaishaku* on his left hand, Taki Zenzaburo advanced slowly towards the Japanese witnesses, and the two bowed before them, then drawing near to the foreigners they saluted us in the same way, perhaps even with more deference; in each case the salutation was ceremoniously returned. Slowly and with great dignity the condemned man mounted on to the raised floor, prostrated himself before the high altar twice, and seated* himself on the felt carpet with his back to the high altar, the *kaishaku* crouching on his left-hand side. One of the three attendant officers then came forward, bearing a stand of the kind used in the temple for offerings, on which, wrapped in paper, lay the *wakizashi*, the short sword or dirk of the Japanese, nine inches and a half in length, with a point and an edge as sharp as a razor's. This he handed, prostrating himself, to the condemned man, who received it reverently, raising it to his head with both hands, and placed it in front of himself.

After another profound obeisance, Taki Zenzaburo, in a voice which betrayed just so much emotion and hesitation as might be expected from a man who is making a painful confession but with no sign of either in his face or manner, spoke as follows:

"I, and I alone, unwarrantably gave the order to fire on the foreigners at Kobe, and again as they tried to escape. For this crime I disembowel myself, and I beg you who are present to do me the honour of witnessing the act."

Bowing once more, the speaker allowed his upper garments to slip down to his girdle, and remained naked to the waist. Carefully, according to custom, he tucked his sleeves under his knees to prevent himself from falling backward; for a noble Japanese gentleman should die falling forwards. Deliberately, with a steady hand he took the dirk that lay before him; he looked at it wistfully, almost affectionately; for a moment he seemed to collect his thoughts for the last time, and then stabbing himself deeply below the waist in the left-hand side, he drew the dirk slowly across to his right side, and turning it in the wound, gave a slight cut upwards. During this sickeningly painful operation he never moved a muscle of his face. When he drew out the dirk, he leaned forward and stretched out his neck; an expression of pain for the first time crossed his face, but he uttered no sound. At that moment the *kaishaku*, who, still crouching by his side, had been keenly watching his every movement, sprang to his feet, poised his sword for a second in the air; there was a flash, a heavy, ugly thud, a crashing fall; with one blow the head had been severed from the body.

A dead silence followed, broken only by the hideous noise of the blood throbbing out of the inert heap before us, which but a moment before had been a brave and chivalrous man. It was horrible.

The *kaishaku* made a low bow, wiped his sword with a piece of paper which he had ready for the purpose, and retired from the raised floor; and the stained dirk was solemnly borne away, a bloody proof of the execution.

The two representatives of the Mikado then left their places, and crossing over to where the foreign witnesses sat, called to us to witness that the sentence of death upon Taki Zenzaburo had been faithfully carried out. The ceremony being at an end, we left the temple.'

* Seated himself—that is in the Japanese fashion, his knees and toes touching the ground and his body resting on his heels. In this position, which is one of respect, he remained until his death.

The reader may think that *Seppuku* is a feudal practice totally removed from the spirit of modern Japan. However, it was only in 1970 that Jukio Mishima, the renowned Japanese author, playwright, nationalist and athletic enthusiast, followed the ancient practice and committed *hara-kiri*. Admiring the traditions of his country, he believed that modern Japan was abandoning its birthright by adopting the customs of the West. Accompanied by his closest supporters he addressed a military assembly and attempted to win their support for a military rising designed to restore Japan to its traditional ways. Failing in this he resorted to the traditional exit of the *Samurai*. On his return to Japan at the end of the second World War, Gogen Yamaguchi, the World's Senior *Goju* instructor, also considered *hara-kiri*. Perhaps the spirit of feudal Japan is considerably nearer the surface than is sometimes supposed.

3 The Dojo

Some books imply that to acquire a competence in Karate all that is needed is to follow the instructions in a good manual and that this can be done from the comfort of one's own home. This is far from true. Books are useful in personal practice but they are not a substitute for good instruction. Practice solely by oneself is not only certain to lead to slow development but probably to a dangerous over-estimation of one's abilities. It can also lead to some anti-social attitudes which would not survive a few sessions in any reputable club. In a good club anyone who thought that Karate was to help him look for trouble in the streets would be very quickly and possibly none too gently shown the door. This reaction is not altogether surprising, as much of Karate's unfortunate image stems directly from individuals who, although never having been inside a *dojo*, have claimed or admitted in court to having used Karate techniques for unlawful purposes. For these reasons it is vital to join a good club. This chapter describes the activities and atmosphere that the newcomer will find on his arrival at the *dojo*—translated as 'Way Place' or place at which one practises one's 'way'. The word *dojo* therefore implies something more than 'gymnasium' with its purely physical connotation.

Unlike the Judo *dojo*, the Karate *dojo* will have a bare wooden floor as throws are the exception rather than the rule and it is easier to move in bare feet on polished non-slip splinterless wood. Dress or *Karategi* consists of a light white suit and a belt, the colour of which indicates the grade of the wearer. Some clubs may wear black *gi*—sometimes this is an indication of a club as interested in publicity gimmicks as in serious training.

The Belt System

The system of coloured belts is possibly one of the reasons for Karate's popularity as it provides an obvious psychological incentive and satisfies the ego of those that strive for and achieve the coveted black belt. It is a Japanese innovation and has not been used, at least until recently, by Chinese styles. The numbers of *Kyu* or student grades varies from association to association,

normally being between 6 and 10 with 1st *Kyu* being the most senior. Some associations have a different coloured belt for each grade whilst others combine two or three grades within the same colour. The following system for example is adopted by the British Karate Kyokushinkai:

White Belt:	Beginners 10th and 9th *Kyus*
Light Blue:	8th and 7th *Kyu*
Yellow:	6th and 5th *Kyu*
Green:	4th and 3rd *Kyu*
Brown:	2nd and 1st *Kyu*

This two grades per colour system is useful in stimulating competition. For example, when a 5th is promoted to 4th *Kyu* he exchanges his yellow for a green belt but he is likely to come into competition with 3rd *Kyus*. As he now wears the same coloured belt as the latter he makes every effort to prove that he is just as good while the 3rd *Kyu* needs to prove that he is genuinely the senior. Both therefore improve through a competitiveness not killed by an over awe of senior grades.

Some associations have fewer than 10 *Kyu* but the fewer there are the more congested the syllabus for each grade becomes. This can cause beginners to get unnecessarily confused and depressed. Until recently the *Kyokushinkai* style had six, rather than 10 grades and it was for this very reason that they changed. The new system also enables them to demand a higher standard of performance for each of the syllabus techniques required in examination.

The *Dan* or black belt grades are graduate as opposed to student grades. The number of grades again varies from association to association with the top man for each major style in the world being an 8th, 9th or 10th *Dan*. Each style operates its own system and these grades are not necessarily comparable. The *Dan* grades run in reverse order to the *Kyu* grades with 10th *Dan* being the highest. The *Dan* grades also have the following courtesy titles which are always used in the *dojo*:

Sempai (senior) — 1st and 2nd *Dans*
If there is no Black belt in the club
the Senior *Kyu* grade will be called *Sempai*.
Sensei (teacher) — 3rd, 4th and 5th *Dans*
Shihan (master) — 6th and 7th *Dans*
Kancho (master of the house) —
This title is reserved for the Senior man
in each of the world-style organisations.

The world's top competition men tend to be about 4th to 5th *Dan* with the more Senior grades being instructors or Honorary grades.

Another very obvious feature of the *dojo* is the use of Japanese terms which can at first rather confuse the beginner. Their use, however, does have several advantages particularly if the club employs a Japanese instructor who is then free to concentrate on technical rather than linguistic matters. Japanese terms are also useful in international competition and reduce the possibility of misunderstandings. To some extent they are also attractive in themselves to many students who are fascinated by most things Japanese. They add a slightly mysterious flavour to what would otherwise be a rather boring system of names.

Unfortunately, however, different styles do sometimes use different names for what amounts to the same technique. In the *Shotokan* style a stamping sideways kick to the knee is known as *Fumikomi*. In the *Kyokushinkai* style it is known as *Kansetu-geri*. When training an all-style national team the use of the home

Use of Japanese terms

language therefore becomes more of a necessity. Even in the single-style club, however, most of the instruction and all of the difficult explanations tend to be in the home language and the use of Japanese terms need not be a deterrent to anyone wishing to take up Karate.

A list of the main Japanese terms used is given in Appendix A.

Japanese etiquette Discipline within the *dojo*, particularly with Japanese instructors, tends to be very strict and the atmosphere formal. The instructor is always addressed as *Sensei* (teacher) or *Shihan* (master) rather than by his name. Surprisingly this formality and discipline seems to appeal to all students almost without exception.

On entering or leaving the *dojo* one would bow towards the main wall on which might hang the association's symbol or, in Japan, would be situated a small Buddhist or Shinto shrine. The bow is a sign of respect—possibly the equivalent of crossing oneself on entering a Catholic church. A bow to the instructor also develops a proper student/teacher relationship.

When the lesson begins, the students line up facing the senior instructors who have their backs to the main wall. On the command *Shindanmirai*, meaning 'We bow to God', the group give a kneeling bow. On the command *Mockso*, meaning 'close eyes', they do so and briefly think upon the meaning of that salutation. Some other styles sit in the *Za Zen* (sitting meditation) position with eyes closed and concentrate on correct posture and breath control, i.e. in at a natural rate and out slowly. This may be continued for quite some time. A similar procedure occurs at the end of the session, with a *dojo* motto or oath possibly being added. One such motto goes as follows:

1. We will train our hearts and bodies for a firm, unshaking spirit.
2. We will pursue the true meaning of the martial way so that, in time, our senses may be alert.
3. With true vigour, we will seek to cultivate a spirit of self-denial.
4. We will observe the rules of courtesy, respect our superiors and refrain from violence.
5. We will follow our gods and Buddha and never forget the virtue of humility.
6. We will look upwards to wisdom and strength, not seeking other desires.
7. All our lives, through the discipline of Karate, we will seek to fulfil the true meaning of the way.

Sentiments such as these coming from a Karate Club often strike the westerner as contradictory and possibly absurd or hypocritical. In most cases this is not so.

A typical training session will last about 90 minutes. There is no set programme and the emphasis will vary according to the style and the subject matter which the instructor wishes to stress. Most sessions, however, are likely to start with warming and stretching exercises, some of which are described in Chapter 4. A beginners' group may then practise their basic technique (*Kihon*) which constitutes, as it were, the grammar of Karate. As teaching methods are very Japanese and formal, great stress is placed upon the proper execution of the basic movements. One of the Senior British instructors trained in Japan spent every night for the first three months practising moving backwards and forwards in the Forward Stance (*Zenkutsu-dachi*) executing only one technique.

These techniques had to be perfected before he was allowed to progress further. Such extremes are rare in the West but this example does indicate the importance generally placed upon basic technique. Techniques are also practised in groups as well as individually. Group training is often accompanied by a shouting chant from the instructor. The shout alternates with that of the students who *Kiai* (shout) in response as they perform the technique. The effect is semi-hypnotic and an instructor experienced in chanting can closely control the timing and effort involved, as can a cox with a rowing crew. Good chanting is very skilled and requires both imagination and a sensitivity to the physical condition of the group. It can enable the instructor to modify the

A typical training session

tempo in such a way as to obtain the maximum possible effort. To lag behind is to lose considerable face and to stop of one's own accord is virtually unheard of. The strengthening effect upon muscle, stamina and determination is therefore considerable. These are some of the reasons why self instruction from a manual cannot possibly be a substitute for joining a good club.

Techniques are also practised individually in front of mirrors, to assist movement analysis. Someone who practises by himself at home in front of a mirror is much more likely to develop a narcissistic tendency to the point where he may actually begin to believe that he is the living embodiment of 007—a very dangerous delusion. Mirrors can, however, be used as an aid to concentration and enable one to watch, analyse and control one's own movement with the mind. It makes one more aware of oneself and therefore gives a greater understanding of that (i.e. oneself) which produces the technique. Through the detailed control involved it develops self-domination—the first essential step to any other form of domination.

A session is also likely to include *Kata*, practised again probably in groups. As groups involve both beginners and experts this is particularly helpful to the former as *Kata* sequences can be very complicated. The sequence can therefore be learned by imitation.

Controlled free fighting in pairs or competition (*Jiu-Kumite*) may also be practised, or strengthening, conditioning or technique improved by use of the bag or the *makiwara*. According to the style of the club, woodbreaking (*Tamashiwari*) may also be performed although this is much less prevalent than is commonly supposed.

One final point is the tremendous team spirit that a good club generates. Some sports like rugby and climbing, due largely to common effort and the dependence of one individual upon another, develop an esprit-de-corp as a matter of course. Karate is in the same category. Having jointly suffered the rigours of a hard training session, a mutual respect, admiration and group loyalty develops. To think of a Karate Club as a social focus may seem to some a little odd but to many *karateka* that is undoubtedly what it is.

Some clubs or associations also occasionally hold *Gashikoos* or training camps. The discipline at such camps might well astound many westerners, although it is as much self imposed as externally imposed. The latter by itself is a sheer waste of time. Particularly with styles that involve strong body contact it may involve a severity that some might consider bordered on brutality. At one such *Gashikoo* when the group took their morning run, an instructor ran behind hitting the last man with a bamboo stick.

During training when some students arrived late or it seemed that they were not working fully, the entire group were again beaten. The aim was not sadism but to create a group feeling and loyalty the like of which can only be generated by mutually shared suffering. Such feeling was traditional to the *Samurai* and is illustrated by the story of the 47 Ronin in Chapter 2. If one suffers, all suffer. The *Gashikoo* aimed to develop that spirit as well as to train the body to accept a certain degree of punishment. Of the 40 students at the camp only one broke down. He cried, said that he had paid to learn Karate not to be beaten and that he was going home. The reply was: 'You are learning Karate—and life—the hard way. And before you do go, leave your black belt.'

Another association had obtained the services of a Buddhist monk during a week's *Gashikoo* and spent a considerable amount of time, particularly with the higher grades, in *Za Zen* (Sitting Meditation). These two illustrations show that the approach of different styles can therefore be considerably different. It is most important for the beginner to know what he is getting into. It is to meet this need that this book is written.

4 Body Conditioning

Irrespective of style, a competent *Karateka* requires a high degree of physical fitness. The following exercises will therefore be of benefit to all. Different styles, however, do stress different aspects of fitness so the emphasis within any particular club is likely to vary. A *Shukokai* club, emphasising competitive sport Karate, would stress speed training whilst stamina training would be less significant. The latter would only be required to produce sufficient strength and speed to last a series of 2–3-minute competitions. Other styles such as *Kyokushinkai* lay greater emphasis upon strength and stamina and there is likely to be more stress upon hard physical conditioning, isometric training and running. In view of the greater contact involved in *Kyokushinkai* competitions a heavier musculature is also required, partly as a certain degree of punishment is accepted in order to enable one to get sufficiently close to deliver a winning blow. *Shotokan* and *Wadoryu* might be said to be in intermediate positions between the two extremes with *Shotokan* inclining towards a power and *Wadoryu* a speed emphasis. *Shotokai* lay particular stress on suppleness and Yoga-type postures are adopted in training.

When practising a particular exercise it is useful to bear in mind its practical application, e.g. leg stretching exercises are essential for high and round-house kicks. To do the exercises mindlessly is likely to lead to an early loss of interest. Training by oneself, however, is neither as enjoyable nor as effective as training in a club. When alone there is a much greater tendency to stop when the going gets hard. In a group the nature of the exercise and the work rate can be controlled by the instructor and all are more prepared to make a maximum effort with the consequent fitness benefits.

The following is a fairly typical club training session. Limber up with stretching exercises for 5 minutes and follow with speed and reaction exercises for a further 10 minutes. The main Karate techniques should then be practised for whatever time is available (varies between one and two hours in most clubs). Complete the session with 10 minutes hard strengthening followed by limbering down.

Limbering up

Karate requires considerable mobility and strength in the joints. The exercises are mainly designed to provide this and to tone up the muscles to prevent injury.

1. EYES   Very gently rub the eyes. To develop all-round vision to the maximum extent, keep the head perfectly still and look as far left then right as possible. Test what objects you can see to the rear. It should be possible to reduce the blind spot to less than a quarter of the full 360° range. Do the same looking upwards and downwards and then rotate the eyeballs through the maximum possible range.

2. NECK   Stand naturally, legs apart. Bend head as far as possible forwards and backwards and from left to right. Now rotate the head in a circular motion. Change direction. This action relaxes the neck and eases tension.

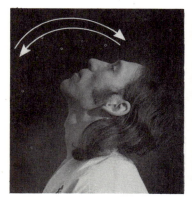
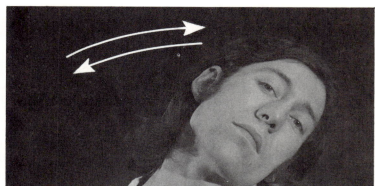
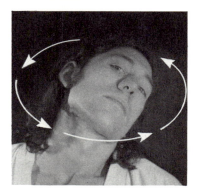

Rotate the arms in big circles in front of the body, then to the side
of the body. Keep the arms straight and the shoulders relaxed.
When circling to the side, press the arms backwards to stretch the
shoulder joint and extend the chest muscles.

3. ARM AND SHOULDER

Feet wide apart. Arms horizontal. Keep feet firm on the ground.
Twist round as far as possible pressing three times with each arm.
In a crowded *dojo* the arms can be bent at the elbows as in the
photograph.

4. TRUNK
a. Trunk twisting

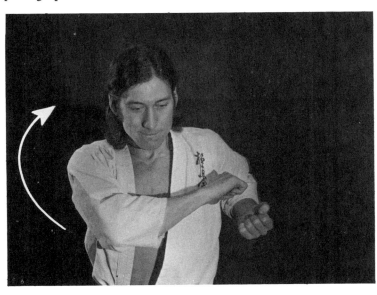

b. Side stretching Feet wide apart. Right arm above head. Left arm by side. Bend to left and then to right stretching with both hands. Press hips forward to prevent bending forward at waist.

c. Trunk rotating (i) Feet wide apart. Keeping the legs straight, stretch forward with both hands and then in a large continuous movement, to the left, backwards and to the right. Repeat circles in alternate directions.

(ii) Sit with left leg forward and right foot tucked over left knee. Place left arm over right side of right knee. Twist head and trunk to right. Reverse foot and leg positions and twist to left.

Feet together. Keeping the legs straight, press down to touch ground with fingers or palms of hands. If necessary spread the feet to make the movement a little easier, but do not bend legs. If very supple grasp the ankles with feet together and gently pull so that the head touches the knees.

5. LEG

a. Stretching ham-strings

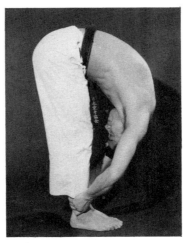

b. Leg swinging forward   Stand with left foot forward. Swing right foot as high as possible. Keep left foot firm on ground. Return right foot to original position. Change legs.

c. Leg swinging sideways   Swing right leg high to side. Get the heel as high as possible and point slightly downwards with the toes.

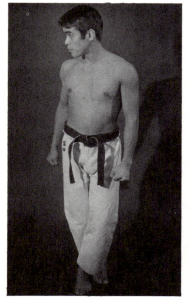

Squat on left foot with right leg out to the side, toes up. Keep foot of supporting leg flat. Hands on knees. Get the buttocks as low as balance permits. Rotating the hips slightly press down on the right knee 3 or 4 times. Repeat with left leg.

d. Knee stretching

Rotate each foot in large circles and stretch the toes.

6. ANKLE AND FOOT

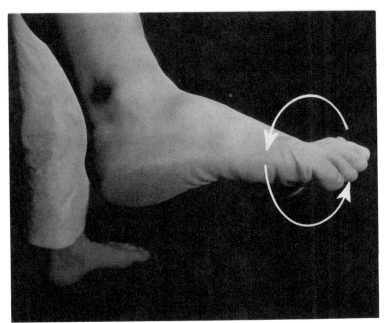

Jog on spot, keeping relaxed and shaking the wrists, knees and ankle joints.

GENERAL

Speed and fast-reaction exercises

a. Light bag   Height can be adjusted to practise a variety of techniques. The heavier the bag the more one develops power as opposed to speed.

b. Suspended tennis ball   Punches and kicks also greatly aids concentration, accuracy and jumping ability.

Ensure that the room has no draughts. Endeavour to punch out the flame by air pressure in front of the fist without actually touching the flame. Start with a thin candle and progress later to a broad one.

c. Candle flame

Hang a sheet of paper, approximately 12 in. from the wall at about head height. Punch with alternate hands as rapidly as possible and endeavour to keep the paper pressed against the wall by air pressure. This should be done without wearing a jacket as the cuffs of the latter will affect air movement.

d. Suspended paper

A few of the world's fastest punchers can punch and withdraw the hand so rapidly that they can push and then pull back the paper by suctional effect alone.

Strengthening exercises

A student practising by himself must estimate for himself the number of repetitions of each exercise that it is advisable to perform. A very useful and cheap publication with progressive exercises is *Physical Fitness* in the Penguin Books series, Number 2055.

a. Push-ups (arm, fingers and shoulder)

Front lying, hands under shoulders, palms flat on floor. Extend arms keeping the body straight. Can be made more difficult by pushing off floor to slap chest with hands before returning to starting position, or by pressing off the tips of two or three fingers only.

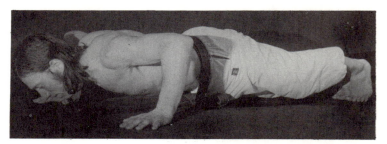

Back lying, hands clasped behind head, feet slightly apart and tucked firmly under something solid or a partner. Sit up rapidly, reaching on alternative lifts with the elbow for the opposite knee.

b. Sit ups (stomach and side)

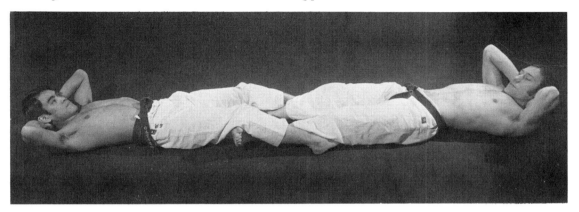

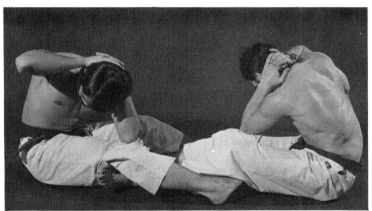

c. Back stretch (*back*)   Front lying, arms clasped behind back. Raise head, chest, legs and thighs off floor and as high as possible. Press back once or twice on each lift. Can be made more difficult by stretching the arms out above the head instead of clasping behind back.

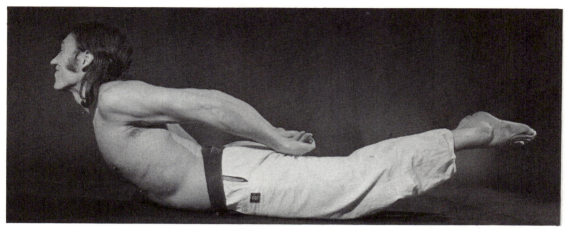

d. Squat walk (*legs*)   Arms behind back, bend knees and squat on flat feet. Keeping knees bent, buttocks low, and back straight, move forwards in a walking action with the legs.

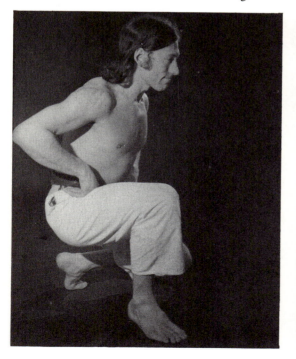

Develops power, toughens the skin, increases the ability of the
joints to withstand shock and is technically useful in developing
the proper relationship between hip and arm movement. Heavy
bags can be used to train all parts of the body, such as fists, palms,
forearms, elbows, shoulders, stomach, hips, knees, feet and head
for striking purposes.

e. Use of Makiwara *and Heavy Bag*

f. Use of bean container   Thrust spear hand into a container of soya beans or, more difficult, fine sand. Pull out the beans with a clawing action of the fingers.

Dangers of callous development

Although toughening of the skin is required to protect the joints and to prevent splitting the skin, the practice of developing large callouses is nowadays both unnecessary and potentially a hazard to health. Due to their historical origins and the need to punch through wooden armour, Okinawan styles tend most to stress callous development. This is now an anachronism. Provided the knuckle is strong, the skin reasonably hard and there is no psychological withdrawal from hitting something hard, the striking power of a calloused and uncalloused hand is virtually the same. Especially in cold damp climates an excessive emphasis on hand toughening can also lead to arthritis in the joints. It is not therefore recommended.

5 The Basic Principles

Psychological

'Know thyself, know thy enemy,
In a hundred battles, a hundred victories'

'To subdue the enemy without even fighting
Is the highest skill of all'
> Sun Szu (Chinese Military Strategist)

A good *karateka*, while not underestimating his opponent, must train himself to instantaneous physical responses and thereby develop self confidence. In addition to physical skills, however, he must also acquire an appropriate mental attitude. First and foremost, he must maintain a state of mental calm and avoid feelings of agitation, fear, anger or any concious concern about defeating his opponent. These will serve merely as distractions and inhibit the proper execution of skills. He should take no notice of attempts by his opponent to distract him. He should in fact be virtually oblivious of any such attempt. The Japanese description of this mental state is to have a 'mind like unruffled water'.

He should also be totally aware of his opponent's movements and the general environment without looking at any particular part of it. He should try to control the total situation rather than concentrate on the execution of individual techniques. To achieve this, many top *karateka* fight with partly closed eyes and slightly furrowed brows, virtually gazing through their opponent into middle distance. Others focus their gaze on only one of their opponent's eyes. The former technique is similar to that used by artists wishing to obscure the superficial elements of a landscape or model in order to concentrate on the major lines. It can also have a very nerve-racking effect upon opponents who find it worrying to be looked at but seemingly to be unnoticed. The technique's main function, however, is to notice everything in proper perspective and not to be distracted by, for example, movements of the hands or eyes. This attitude fits perfectly with the Zen concept of 'no thought' and total immersion in the environment. It also enables one to react appropriately to situations as they occur. One should even be totally receptive to receiving a blow as, by being aware of it, one is better able to absorb it.

With an approach such as this many opponents can be 'psyched', almost hypnotised, into defeat. The highest skill is, after all, to subdue the enemy without even fighting. The logical development of this attitude is that one subdues the other by his mere presence. It is perhaps interesting to note that in Chinese script the character for 'bu' in 'budo' (fighting way) is actually that for 'stop' written inside the character representing two crossed halberds (combined spear and battle axe). The ideal of the 'fighting way' is therefore to prevent a fight or even a confrontation before it occurs. Where there is no confrontation, there is no victor and no vanquished and where there is no vanquished there are no seeds for a future confrontation.

A more detailed analysis of the psychology of competition can be found under 'Free Fighting Tactics'.

1. Physical

1. *Stance* (*Dachi*)
Stance relates to the position of the lower body and is vital in that it is the foundation upon which the entire superstructure of stability, balance, mobility, generation of power and control is based. It would be a mistake to assume that it is merely an insignificant foot position incidental to actual fighting. This attitude could be as dangerous as putting radial tyres on the front and cross-ply on the back wheels of a car. Anything might happen and probably would. The feet provide traction as do good tyres. They are not just placed or pressed onto the ground but by a twisting action provide friction and therefore stability. Each stance is a living thing with its own isometrics, applications, advantages and disadvantages. It is for this reason that instructors say 'before you learn to fight, learn to stand'. A bad stance inevitably results in poorly executed techniques.

All Karate styles without exception, therefore, stress it from the start and subsequently continue to practise individual stances whilst also practising the basic kicks and strikes. Unlike boxers, who tend to move about lightly with their centre of gravity fairly high, *karateka* generally move with a lower centre of gravity, adopting a series of recognisable foot and leg positions. Top-class competition *karateka* may very occasionally dance about as do boxers, but on striking or kicking they drop into a recognisable stance suited to the technique which they are about to perform and from which they can obtain maximum power. They recognise that, as with a tree, the source of strength lies in the roots not in the branches.

Descriptions of all stances and variations adopted by all or even just the major styles, would be impractical to incorporate in any one book. The following have been chosen as with very minor modifications they are common to all styles and provide a basic repertoire from which attacks can be launched in all directions. Stances with a wide base and a low centre of gravity (i.e. Forward and Straddle stances) are suited to powerful punching while those with a higher centre of gravity (Cat stance) are designed for mobility and speed of action. There is no stance suited to all situations.

The key to the diagrams is as follows:

 ⟵——— Effective punching or kicking direction
 ← – – Direction of leg tension
 —•— Line of hips with position of centre of gravity

N.B.: In all instances the upper body is vertical. Boxes indicate size of base and degree of stability.

Ready or Open Leg stance
(*Hachiji-dachi*)

This is merely a natural posture from which one can move into any of the following combat stances. You should therefore practise moving from it into each of these stances as well as from one stance into another.

Forward stance
(*Zenkutsu-dachi*)

The feet are approximately twice the shoulder width apart and the body faces forward. The rear leg is tensed with the heel as flat as possible and the foot pointing about 45° to the front. The hips are low and the ankle and knee joints should be tensed in an outward direction. The back should be straight and the head up. The centre of gravity is rather closer to the front than the rear foot creating a strong defensive position to the front, well suited to techniques such as *age-uke* (upper block).

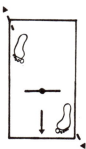

This is a defensive position in which 70 per cent of the weight is on the rear leg. The hips are turned at 45° while the rear leg is well bent, with the foot pointing sideways. The legs are tensed in an outward direction. As there is little weight on the front foot, this leg can be easily used. By moving the centre of gravity forward the body can also be moved toward the opponent enabling counter attacks by, for example, *Gyaku-Zuki* (counter punch with rear hand).

Backward stance (*Kotutsu-dachi*)

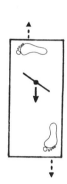

This stance is named after its obvious similarity to a horse riding position. Both feet are firmly on the ground and point forward. It is executed with the foot space varying from shoulder to twice shoulder width apart, although most styles stress the latter. The weight is evenly distributed on both feet and the leg, buttock and back muscles are tightened pressing the knees in an outward direction. This stance is suited to the delivery of strong sideway techniques such as the backfist strike (*riken-uchi*).

Horse or Straddle stance (*Kiba-dachi*)

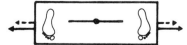

Diagonal Horse or Diagonal Straddle stance (Sochin-dachi)

This is the horse stance twisted sideways. The hips still face forward but the foot position is angled at about 45°. The weight remains evenly distributed on both feet. With a wide base this is a very strong attacking and defensive stance permitting thrusts in all directions. Unlike the Hourglass stance, which it superficially resembles, knee pressure is in an outward direction.

Hourglass stances

Both feet point at an angle of 45° to the front and are placed about twice shoulder width apart (*Hangetsu-dachi*). The body weight is evenly distributed on both feet. Hips face forward and the inward pressure of the knees enables a strong sideways thrust suitable to the execution of the backfist strike (*riken-uchi*).

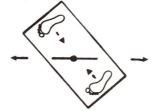

When performed from a narrower base (i.e.: about shoulder width apart) (*Sanchin-dachi*) the rear foot tends to toe-in and point forwards. The toes of the front foot and the toes of the rear foot should be almost in line with the heel of the front foot.

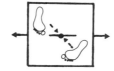

Ninety per cent of the weight is on the rear foot. The front foot is poised lightly on the ball and is in line with the heel of the rear foot. The knee of the front leg points directly forward with the thigh in a good position to defend the groin. This stance facilitates quick changes in position. It is often used in competition. It is also for performing *Kin-geri* (groin kick) and other attacks with the front foot.

Cat stance (*Neko-ashi-dachi*)

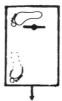

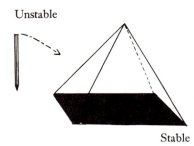

Unstable

Stable

2. Balance and movement

To stand a pencil on its tip is virtually impossible, but to stand a pyramid-shaped block on its base is extremely easy. This is because it is not feasible to place the pencil's centre of gravity above or within its base, i.e. the point of contact with the ground. In the case of the pyramid this presents no problem. The bigger the base and the lower the centre of gravity the more difficult it is for the block to be overturned.

The same principle applies to Karate stances. In other words the Horse stance or the Forward stance are considerably more stable than the Cat stance, in which the centre of gravity is not only high but the base is very small. Compare boxed areas of diagrams on pages 50 and 53.

Stability is obviously a desirable objective but to strive to lower the centre of gravity unduly would be to sacrifice mobility. One basic reason for the existence of many different styles of Karate is the different emphasis placed upon the importance of stability and mobility. The *Shotokan Karateka* for example can often be recognised by his use of broad stances and powerful punching positions which exploit hip rotation to the maximum possible extent. The *Shukokai* specialist is likely to fight with a higher centre of gravity possibly sacrificing some stability for speed and manoeuvrability. At least one South Chinese style is based mainly on the Cat stance and relies not on stability and hard counters but on spinning body movement, deflections of opponent's attacks and very rapid spring-like counters. It might be said to operate on the principle of a spinning top, rather than a stable pyramid—if the right-hand side is attacked the fighter spins away on that side, possibly attacking with the left foot whilst employing *Aikido*-like clutching techniques on the right, to unbalance his opponent. Mobility has assumed almost total precedence over stability. These points should be borne in mind by anyone presented with a choice of practising one style or another. Many individuals are likely to have physical characteristics, i.e. great speed or strength, making one style personally more appropriate. Provided all other things are equal, i.e. quality of instructor, etc., this could well be the deciding factor.

In practising, forward or backward movement or movement from one stance to another, the following general points should be remembered:
1. Hips should move first with a rotary movement, followed by the legs. Arms move last.
2. The hips should not move up and down.
3. The feet should move close to the ground.
4. All movements should be performed smoothly.

5. The appropriate direction of leg tensions should be applied when the new positions are adopted.

Methods of moving for the various stances previously described are listed below.

Movement for Forward stance (Zenkutsu-dachi)

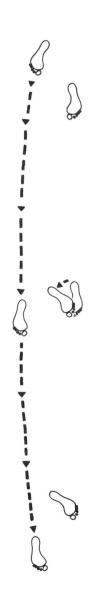

The stationary foot should be kept firmly on the ground. The moving foot should move close to the ground passing close to the front foot in a slight inward arc. This permits a possible defence of the groin by means of the thigh. When moving backwards, bend the rear knee first then glide the front foot to the rear.

When practising a 180° turn, the rear foot should be moved sideways behind the body, about the width of the shoulders. The body should then be pivoted on the balls of the feet to face the opposite direction.

Forward and backward movements for these stances are basically similar to those described for the Forward stance, although the foot positions are as described in the relevant section.

In moving sideways, bring the left foot in front of the right foot and place close alongside. Legs should be slightly bent, the hips low and the upper body straight. The right foot should then be moved behind the left about two shoulder widths distant. The movement should be performed smoothly.

Movement for Backward stance/ Diagonal Horse or Straddle stance/Hour Glass stance

Movement for Horse stance

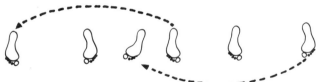

Movement for Cat stance   In moving forward the weight is moved from the rear to the front foot. The rear foot then moves straight forward enabling the thigh to protect the groin and the new rear foot pivots to an angle of 45°. Moving backwards is the reverse process.

As stated previously, the beginner should practise moving from one stance to another by pivoting the hips and sliding rather than lifting the feet to the appropriate position. He should also stand in the natural position (i.e. feet 3 in. or 4 in. apart) and practise quickly adopting each of the various stances.

3. Development of power

Demonstrations of *Tamashiwari* (Wood breaking) can be so impressive that, quite often, spectators assume that they contain an element of trickery. This is not so. It is merely a question of concentrating one's entire strength in the proper place at the proper time, though proper co-ordination of the body's resources, and having a sufficiently hardened hand for this to be psychologically and physically possible.

Force or power has been defined as 'mass times the square of the velocity'. Obviously there is relatively little that one can do about one's mass except to ensure that it is firmly positioned and capable of withstanding impact. Speed, however, is vitally important and in it relaxation plays a significant part.

4. Relaxation

Tense muscles are incapable of rapid movement. To develop speed it is therefore necessary to keep the body relaxed as long as possible. Tensing should only occur immediately before impact.

The most complete muscular relaxation is normally possible directly following total tension. Relaxation can therefore be learnt by tensing and then relaxing the body. One of the aims of the very tense *Sanchin Kata* is to develop relaxation in this way.

5. Use of hips

The muscles of the legs and hips are far stronger than those of the arm. As the speed of a whip is generated by the handle so the speed of the hand is generated by the legs and hips, which serve as its base. It is quite impossible to throw a fast powerful punch with arm and shoulder strength alone. To increase the power and speed of a punch you should always endeavour to bring the maximum number of muscles into play by rotating the hips faster. Although the hips are a convenient point upon which to concentrate, it is actually the entire hip, thigh and side of the body on the side of the striking arm that should generate speed by rotating around its point of axis, which is down the centre of the body. This momentum is then transmitted via the shoulder to the arm which accelerates as more and more muscles are brought into play. By the point of focus, with proper co-ordination, the fist can have developed quite remarkable speed. It should, of course, be remembered that a chain is only as strong as its weakest link and that failure in any part of the technique can cause a break in the transmission of power.

Different styles do use the hips in different ways but all recognise its importance. *Shotokan karateka* for example tend to fight with broad stances and the hips diagonal to the opponent, thus

Shotokan   Wadoryu   Shukokai

permitting pronounced hip rotation and use of the leg. *Shukokai* Karate, however, which emphasises speed rather than power, tends to adopt narrower stances with the hips squarer to the opponent. This does not permit such extensive hip movement but power is nevertheless generated by a spring-like double movement of the hips, which are withdrawn and rebound forward as would a spring under tension. The faster the backward movement the faster the recoil forward movement. The *Wadoryu* position is a cross between the two with the technique nearer *Shukokai* than *Shotokan*, although the hips are not so square to the opponent.

6. Breathing and Kiai

Breathing plays an important part in all the martial arts including Karate. The *Goju 'Sanchin' Kata*, for example, assists the development of both relaxation and tension and creates an understanding of the relationship between breathing and movement. In training, one should be conscious of the breathing technique but in performance or in competition one should be completely oblivious of it. The effect of strong *Sanchin* breathing can become self hypnotic and the performer can become totally identified with his own movement rather than any individual aspect of it.

Relaxed

By expelling air in the form of a *Kiai* or yell, one can gather one's fighting spirit, assist muscle contraction and create a psychological focus for the blow. It is as if the breathing action unifies the mental and the physical both in preparation for and the application of combat. It can also quite possibly terrify the opponent or at least momentarily unbalance him, thus providing an opening for attack. In general, one relaxes while inhaling through the nose and exhaling with a *Kiai*, normally through the mouth. Some styles, particularly *Goju*, cut off the expulsion of air and therefore the noise at the moment of focus by ramming the tongue behind the teeth with the mouth closed. They consider that this action adds further to tension on focus. You should also use the type of abdominal breathing adopted by Yogi and, to a less extent opera singers. With this you have the physical sensation of breathing air into the abdominal region. All the martial arts place great emphasis on abdominal breathing and Orientals believe the abdomen to be the source of strength as well as life. Gogen Yamaguchi, the world's leading *Goju* exponent, is also a Yoga practitioner and has adapted Yoga (*Pranayama*) breathing techniques for his own purpose. As explained in Chapter One, breathing can also be used to ensure a state of mental calm, although this requires considerable skill and control to be effective.

With Kiai

7. Focus

If the body has been kept relaxed in executing a punch, the drive of the legs, hips, trunk and arm properly used, and breathing and *Kiai* well timed, the fist will be moving very fast immediately prior to impact. The entire body must then instantaneously tense, joints locking, concentrating the total energy for a split second on the target point. It is by this tensing that speed is transformed into power. This is the meaning of 'focus'. It lasts only for an instant and is immediately followed by relaxation and adoption of the posture appropriate to the next technique.

8. Distance

To be the correct distance from the opponent is extremely important, but the actual distance will vary from individual to individual. A big strong man may well choose to fight up close, being prepared to accept blows in order to be able to deliver a particularly hard one. The *Kyokushinkai* style place great emphasis on body conditioning in order to be able to do just this. A small fast moving man on the other hand might be advised to fight from a distance, moving quickly in attack and retreat. To be lured into a close fighting position could be disastrous. The ideal position is one from which you can attack, block and follow up without affecting body balance.

9. Understanding

To really master any movement, it is necessary to understand all the elements that go to comprise it. For example, speed is largely the product of relaxation and explosiveness. For an instructor merely to shout 'Faster, Faster' is not particularly helpful unless one knows how to do it. You should try, therefore, to understand a movement right down to its roots. Ask questions and hope for answers that make sense. An instructor who does not wish to answer, creates an atmosphere of mystique, or superficial ritual or says that you will know for yourself in five years' time, is likely not to know the answer himself or is deliberately retarding progress, probably for financial reasons. In either case the solution is quite simple—find an instructor who is open-minded and whose motives are genuine. And, finally, do not stop thinking for yourself.

6 Fighting Techniques

Parts of the body used as weapons
The part of the body most frequently used for striking is the fist.
It is therefore important that it should be correctly formed. An
incorrectly formed fist can result in injury to the fingers or wrist.
The fingers should be clenched tightly and firmly locked with the
thumb which folds over the first and middle fingers. A tight fist
will also enable the wrist to be locked.

Fist
Forefist (Seiken)

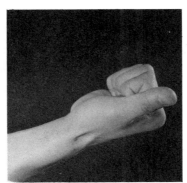

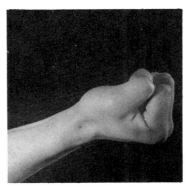

The striking point is the knuckles of the first and middle finger. This relatively small point of contact provides a greater concentration of force than would be obtained by striking with the entire surface of the fist. On striking, the elbow, wrist, knuckles and point of contact should all be in a straight line.

 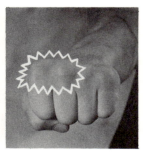

Backfist strike (*Uraken*) The fist formation is similar to that for the forefist, although the wrist is slightly bent. This strike is useful for attacks to the left and right.

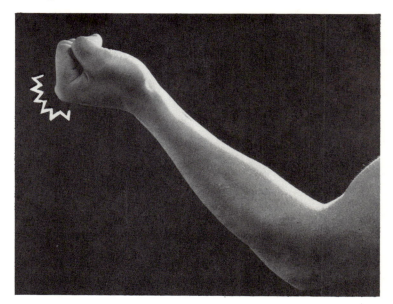

Extend the knuckle of the middle finger. Clench tight with the thumb. Used to attack the temple, solar plexus and other points.

Middle finger, one knuckle fist (*Nakadate ippon Ken*)

All fingers are extended with the thumb in line. Attempt to get the tips of the three striking fingers in line. This involves the fingers being slightly bent. Used in attacks to soft parts of the body especially the abdomen and neck.

Fingers
Spear hand (*Nukite*)

Variations on this attack involve extension of the first and second fingers only. In self defence this may be used in attacks to the eyes.

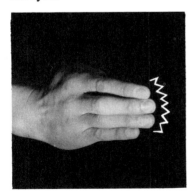

Knife hand (*Shuto*)   Extend the fingers and thumb with a very slight curve in the palm of the hand. Used for attacks to the face and abdominal region and also for blocks. In *Tamashiwara* the point of contact is the joint at the base of the outside edge of the hand, rather than the entire side of the hand.

Palm heel (*Teisho*)   The wrist is bent well back. Used mainly to attack the face and stomach and sometimes in blocking.

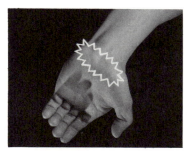

Elbow (*Empi*)   Can be used as a powerful weapon in forward, backward, sideways and upward attacks.

Useful in backward kicks. When restrained from the rear, can be used to attack the instep, shin or groin.

Foot
Heel (Kakato)

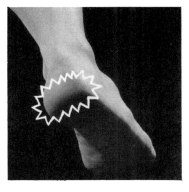

Used in sidekicks to the upper body, armpit and knee.

Knife foot (Sokuto)

Bend the toes upwards as far as possible. This strengthens the ball and prevents injury to the toes. Used in roundhouse and front kicks.

Ball of the foot (Koshi)

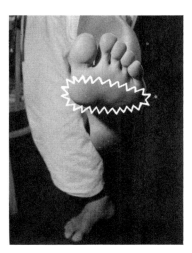

Instep (Haisoku)   Press toes downwards and keep together. Used to attack groin and roundhouse kicks to the head or ribs.

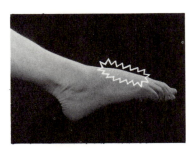

Knee (Hiza)   Used to attack groin, abdomen or face against an attacker who moves in low or attempts a head butt.

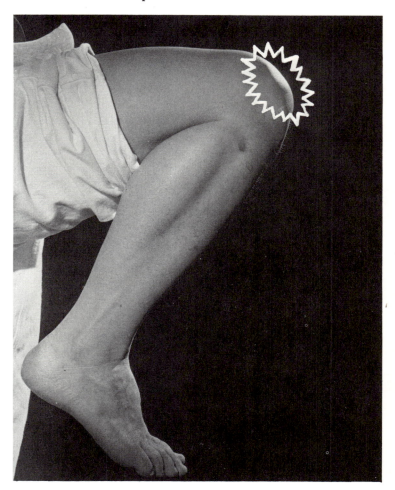

Punching, striking and thrusting

At first sight the words 'punch', 'strike' and 'thrust' appear to be synonymous. In Karate, however, they have different and precise meanings. A punch relates to a blow in which the fist moves in a straight line from the start of the punch to the point of focus. A thrust is also in a straight line but contact is made with the point of the finger or fingers rather than the fist. A strike involves a rotary movement of the hand and forearm and a snapping action at the elbow. The difference between a strike and the other two might be likened to a slashing action with a knife as compared to a stab. For convenience all the following blows have been classified according to the part of the body with which the blow is made. It will be clear from the names, however, into which of the three categories they fall.

Bottom left: Thrust
Below left: Strike
Below right: Punch

When practising punching, remember the basic physical principles such as relaxation, use of hips, breathing and *kiai*, and how to develop power as described in Chapter 5. Most practices are described for blows with the right hand. They can, of course, be practised with the left by substituting 'left' for 'right' as appropriate.

Forefist straight punch (Seiken)   The most commonly used punching technique is the forefist straight punch (*Seiken*) directed at the face or middle body. To practise this punch with alternate hands, stand in the Open Leg or Straddle/Horse stance with the left arm forward and the right fist withdrawn above the hip, thumb up. Punch straight and fast towards the opponent's face or abdomen, rotating the wrist and forearm to focus on contact with the knuckles up. The wrist should be firm and straight. The rotating action adds power and accuracy to the punch. Do not totally straighten the arm on contact as it can have a jarring effect upon the elbow. While punching with the right fist withdraw the left forcefully, to the ready position, thumb up.

Applications of the forefist straight punch
1. Reverse punch (Gyaku–Zuki)   This punch requires no foot movement. It is therefore very fast and well suited to counter-punching and point scoring in competition. It is necessary to be close to the opponent to deliver this punch. Stand in the forward stance, left foot and hand forward, right hand by right hip. Most styles would have the hips angled at about 45° to the front. Keeping the elbow in and rotating the fist, punch towards the abdomen or face. The elbow position

provides control and makes the blow more difficult to block. Keep the body upright and pull back the left elbow and fist forcefully.

Similar to the reverse punch, except that the right foot slides forward. As the step brings one nearer to the opponent this technique is useful when the opponent is too distant for *Gyaku-zuki*. Stand in the left forward stance. Slide rather than step forward quickly with the right foot. There is some slight difference of opinion as to when the punch should start. As the most common error among beginners is to start too soon it is therefore wise to delay it as long as possible. Do not start to punch until the right foot is firm. This provides a stable position. Keep the left heel flat on the ground and do not lean forward.

2. Lunge punch (Oi-Zuki)

Backfist strike (Uraken)   A good surprise technique that can be used to strike forward, sideways or to the rear. It involves a fast snapping action of the wrist, forearm and elbow and the first moves in an arc rather than a straight line. Normally used in in-fighting and aimed at soft parts of the body such as the face, groin or solar plexus. Contact is with the back of the first and second knuckle. To avoid injury to the elbow do not fully straighten the arm. When practising striking forward, stand in the forward or diagonal straddle stance with the fists in front of the chest. Strike to the face, knuckles sideways, keeping the elbow near the centre line of the body. A snap of the wrist should be added at the end of the movement.

Roundhouse strike (Mawashi-zuki)   Stand in the left forward stance, the left hand forward, the right fist positioned by the right hip or the small of the back. The latter position enables more power to be applied. Strike towards the opponent's left temple. The fist and forearm rotate anti-clockwise, so that the back of the first and second knuckles, moving in an arc, strike the temple from the side. Withdraw the left arm quickly.

 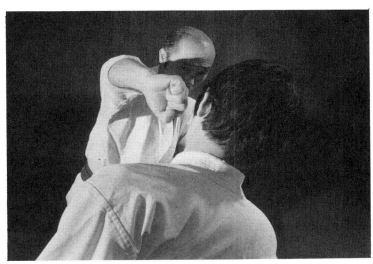

The fast snapping elbow action is similar to that for the back fist strike, except that contact is with the bottom fleshy part of the fist. The action is similar to using a hammer. Used to strike downwards or sideways particularly at joints or hard surfaces, such as the head or shoulder blades.

Hammer fist (Tettsiu-uchi)

Palm heel thrust (*Teisho-tsuki*)   Used both as an attack and as a block to punches or kicks. Stand in the left forward stance, left hand forward right hand by the right side, knuckles down. Thrust forward and upward rotating the wrist and forearm through 180°. Thrust towards the jaw or the bridge of the nose with the heel of the palm, fingers pointing up. This technique can also be used sideways towards the ribs.

Used to strike opponent's temple, collar-bone or neck. Stand in left forward stance, left arm forward right hand by the right ear. Strike forward in a slight arc towards the left temple or neck, rotating the wrist so that contact is from the side with the knife hand, palm up. Power comes from the hips and the snapping action of the elbow and wrist. Withdraw the left hand simultaneously. When striking to the collar-bone the movement is in a downward direction.

Knife hand strike (Shuto)

Spear hand thrust (*Nukite*)   This sharp thrusting action is used to attack soft parts of the body such as eyes, throat or the solar plexus. Do not fully straighten the arm. Contact is with the tips of the middle three fingers, the palm pointing upwards, sideways or downwards. In attacks to the eyes, two or one finger attacks can be used.

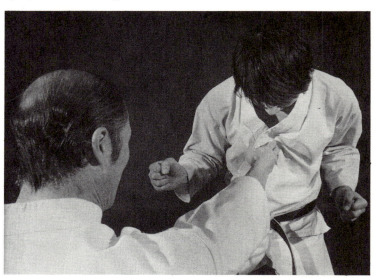

This powerful, close in-fighting, technique can be used to strike forward to the jaw or the solar plexus, sideways or backwards to the ribs, or downwards to a fallen opponent. When held from the rear a backward strike with the right elbow can be accompanied by a hooked punch with the left fist over the right shoulder to the face of the adversary.

Elbow strike (Empi-uchi)

Blocking (Uke)

It has been said that a good *karateka* will never strike first. This statement, however, reflects a technical as well as a moral attitude, which is illustrated by the number of top *karateka* who are primarily counter-punchers. They are this for technical advantage rather than from a moral standpoint, although they would doubtless also agree with that standpoint. Blocks and attacks are two sides of the same coin and a properly executed block should place one in a good position for an effective attack. A fully 'focused' block can itself be an attack and be so painful as to deter any subsequent assaults.

Most blocks are performed with the hands and fall into two broad categories: hard, straight blocks and softer deflecting blocks. Most blocks fall between the two extremes. Any block which is delivered in exactly the opposite direction to the line of attack will result in a hard collision and probable injury to both parties. In its extreme form it does not therefore occur. All blocks consequently contain an element of deflection and are based on the principle of circular movement, with the rotation being around the shoulder, elbow and possibly the wrist. In general, attacks to the face are deflected upwards, those to the body sideways and those to the groin downwards.

In applying a fully 'focused' block the same general principles apply as in a punch, i.e. maintenance of balance, use of relaxation, hips and *kiai*. It can in fact be thought of as a strike at an approaching limb rather than merely as a block. The longer the route the blocking arm travels the greater also will be its power on impact. Timing, therefore, is of paramount importance. Styles placing emphasis upon fully 'focused' blocks include *Shotokan*. Softer deflections using the hand as well as the arm and emphasising speed and counter punching are employed by *Wadoryu* and some of the Chinese styles. The following are some of the basic blocks.

Used as a 'focused' block to attacks to the face, deflecting the attacking arm above head height. Stand in a 'forward stance' with the right foot and left hand forward and the right fist by the right hip. The right (blocking) arm is thrust upwards, moving close to the body, and rotating so that the block is made with the outer surface of the forearm. The elbow is bent at approximately 90°. Contact is focused at forehead height.

Upper level rising block (Jodan Age-uke)

Whilst performing the block the left hand is pulled back strongly with a twisting movement to the hips, knuckles facing down. This adds power to the blocking arm.

Forearm blocks (Udi-uke) Used to protect the chest and stomach area and to deflect blows to the side. Often used from the 'forward stance'.

1. *Middle outside forearm block (Chudan Udi-uke)* Stand in the 'forward stance' right foot forward with the right fist near the ear, elbow out. Swing the elbow across the body in a slight downward arc, rotating the wrist so that the block is made with the outer surface of the forearm near the wrist. Focus on impact. Pull the left hand back as with *Jodan Age-uke* above.

Stand in the forward stance right foot forward, with the right fist by the left armpit. Swing the blocking arm forward and slightly upwards, using the elbow as a fulcrum. Rotate the wrist so that the block is made with the inner surface of the forearm near the wrist. Focus on impact. Pull the left hand back as with *Jodan Age-uke*.

2. *Middle inside forearm block (Chudan Uchi-uke)*

3. *Downward block* (*Gedan Barai*)   Used primarily against kicks and punches to the abdomen or groin. Stand in a 'forward stance', right foot forward with the right hand by the left ear. Sweep the right arm in a forward and downward direction, rotating the wrist. Contact is made with the outer surface of the forearm near the wrist with the arm fully extended. Focus about 8–10 inches in front of the right thigh. Pull the left arm back as with *Jodan Age-uke*.

A useful self-defence technique usable in downward and upward directions. Rarely used in competition.

Cross blocks (*Juji-uke*)

From chest height thrust both arms upwards, palms forward and hands open, deflecting the punch upwards at a point about 12 in. in front of the face. The open hands permit grasping the opponent's wrist in counter-attack and might possibly lead to a kick to the groin. Clenched fist blocks are stronger but require greater accuracy and do not so easily lead to follow up attacks.

1. *Upward block*

2. Downward block A similar technique can be used to block kicks to the groin. To avoid damage to the fingers the fists should be clenched. At the moment of blocking, the opponent should be fairly close and the block might be followed with a double hand attack to the neck.

Kicking (Geri)

The leg, being larger than the arm, is capable of much greater striking power. Its speed is, however, slower and the distance over which it travels generally longer than that of the arm. Certain kicks in particular (i.e. *mawashi-geri*) are therefore more prone to blocks and counters. The leg may also be grabbed or the support leg swept away. Kicks should therefore be as fast as possible and foot withdrawal immediate.

As all kicks, with the exception of jumping kicks are performed on one foot only, balance is most important. The standing foot should be strongly positioned in relation to the direction of thrust and, as far as possible, the body should be kept perpendicular to the ground. Leaning backwards will not only affect balance but will also reduce kicking power. Leaning forward will affect balance and will bring the upper body more within striking range of the opponent. To ensure stability on contact the standing leg should be slightly bent and firm so that the shock can be absorbed at the ankle, knee and hip. To obtain maximum power attempt to kick with the entire body rather than the leg alone.

This is the simplest kick and is performed with the ball of the foot, toes curled upward to avoid injury. Stand in the left forward stance. Pull the right knee to the chest, leg bent, and snap the lower leg forward towards the opponent's abdomen. The knee lift provides speed as the leg therefore moves on a shorter axis. The supporting foot should be flat, the leg slightly bent at the knee. Thrust the hips forward whilst keeping the body vertical. To prevent the leg being grabbed, bend the knee after contact and withdraw to the original stance. This action should be immediate and of a rebound nature. A common mistake is to drop the kicking foot to the ground in front of the support foot. This leaves you vulnerable to leg sweeps.

Front kick (Mae-geri)

Groin kick (*Kin-geri*)   This is basically similar to the front kick except that the toes are pointed down and contact is made with the top of the foot. The kicking action is a flick from the knee rather than a hard driving thrust. It is not used in competition.

Side kick (*Yoko-geri*)   This kick can be performed with a snapping action of the knee when it is aimed at soft parts of the body (such as the abdomen or neck) or as a straight sideways thrust (when it is aimed at bonier parts, such as the knee, ribs or chin).

Stand in either the natural or the forward position and lift the kicking foot to knee height. Use the knife edge or the heel with which to strike. For snap kicks develop a sideways flicking action from the knee, but do not fully extend the leg as this could result in injury to the knee. For thrusts, kick hard in a straight line, tense the hips and fully extend the leg. In both cases toes should be turned down to avoid injury, the heel should protrude and the leg should be withdrawn quickly. Some styles bend the big toe up in order to tense the muscles of the foot and help protrude the heel. For high kicks considerable flexibility must be developed.

Back kick (*Ushiro-geri*) This long-range attack is the only kick in which the body does not remain vertical. Stand in the ready position and raise the kicking leg, bent at the knee, as for *mae-geri*. Dropping the body forward, kick backwards with the heel, toes curled up, towards the groin, stomach or chest. Look over or under the shoulder towards the target. Snap the leg back quickly after contact.

A more advanced practice can be used to attack an opponent standing in front. Stand in the forward stance, left foot forward. Move the right foot sideways behind the left foot, rotate on the balls of the feet to face the opposite direction and turn the head to look over the right shoulder. Kick back with the right foot. This two-part movement can also be combined into a single movement, rotating solely on the ball of the left foot.

Stand in the left forward stance. Bend the right knee and ankle and swing the leg upwards and sideways in a half circular movement to strike towards the temple, neck or ribs with the ball of the foot. Pivoting slightly on the support foot, swing the hips and add a snapping movement of the knee just prior to contact. Attempt to make the direction of the kicking arc and the toes point slightly down on contact. So far as possible, the body should remain upright and half turned to the front. Return the foot quickly to the original stance.

Roundhouse kick (mawashi-geri)

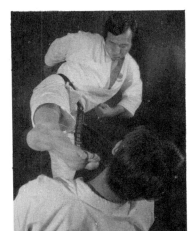

To be performed properly this kick requires considerable flexibility. In the first instance, especially for kicks to the neck, it is also easier to practise it by striking with the instep rather than the ball of the foot. If striking the head, however, this could result in injury to the foot.

Knee kick (*Hiza-geri*) Used in close fighting to attack the groin, ribs or in the case of someone attacking low, the face. The drive may be directly forward and upward or in a semi-circular movement.

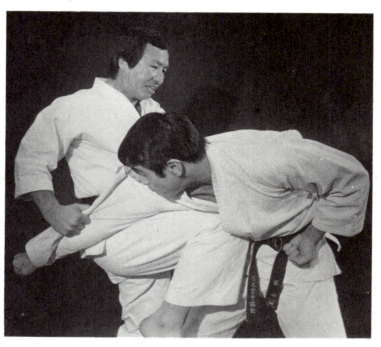

Heel kick (*Fumikomi*) This kick with the heel can be used to stamp forward, sideways or backwards to the opponent's knee, shin or instep. It is particularly useful when held from the rear.

Throwing

Being primarily a punching and kicking art, throws do not figure prominently within Karate. Unlike Judo, where a good throw is an end in itself, in Karate it is merely a means of unbalancing the opponent in order to deliver a fully focused blow. However perfectly a throw is performed in competition it will not receive a point unless followed up. Most Judo throws also involve holding and grappling and therefore necessitate a close body position. Such throws are unsuitable to Karate as they are within striking range.

Because it can be used from a distance and does not involve holding, the most commonly used throw in Karate is *De-Ashi-Barai*. If the opponent is standing with his left foot forward the aim is to sweep away the leg with your right foot causing him to fall heavily on his back. You can then immediately follow with a straight downward punch to the head or whatever other part of the body presents itself.

De-Ashi-Barai

Stand in the left forward stance, facing your opponent in the same position. Move the right foot quickly forward in a slight arc to sweep the opponent's foot behind the heel. Contact is made with the sole of the foot. The movement must be fast and well timed to catch the opponent unprepared. The degree to which the supporting leg is bent depends upon the distance from the opponent. The further he is the greater the bend. The attacking leg should be straight with the knee firm. The opponent's leg is swept forward in a diagonal direction causing him to fall on his back. Move forward and controlling the opponent with the left hand, strike down with the right.

Practice fighting

All the techniques described earlier in this book can and should, in the first instance, be practised individually. However, when the basic skill has been acquired it is necessary to move onto more realistic training with an opponent. Graded forms of practice fighting have therefore been devised to enable a steady progression to the final most realistic form of free fighting (*Jiu-kumite*). A beginner should not try to free fight too soon. It is both detrimental to progress and dangerous.

One-step sparring

Two opponents face each other having previously decided who will attack and who will defend. The specific type of attack, defence and counter-attack, is also pre-determined. There is therefore no real element of surprise and both can concentrate on their technique so that it becomes automatic. The attacker moves one pace forward in executing his move. This sparring is invaluable for developing a sense of distance, timing and for sharpening the reflexes. It should be practised several times before exchanging roles.

Three or five-step sparring

One-step sparring can be developed further so that the attacker launches a set series of attacks each of which are blocked in a specific way with a counter being applied only after the final punch, kick or strike.

Semi-free style sparring

Again the attacker, the defender and the blows are specified but the two move about freely with the former looking for an opening. This again develops a sense of distance and timing and is midway towards free fighting.

Free fighting

This is the most highly developed and realistic form of Karate and is used for competition. It is covered in detail in Chapter 9.

7 Kata

The general publication of combat techniques in book form is a 20th century innovation. Techniques were originally passed down by personal example and word of mouth and were treated with great secrecy. Because of the lack of easy reference it was therefore necessary to devise a system which would enable techniques to be remembered and practised when the instructor was not present. By combining them in a fixed sequence this could be achieved. A *Kata* is therefore designed to assist practice and takes the form of imaginary fighting with several attackers approaching from different directions.

There are in all well over fifty *Kata* of one style or another, many old, some modern and all ranging in complexity and length. In several instances the *Kata* practised by individual styles are only slight variations on those of other styles. This is because they stem from a common source. Each style normally has about five basic *Kata*, which cover all the basic techniques and numerous other advanced *Katas*. For example, the most basic *Shotokan Kata* is *Taikyoku Shodan* (First Cause) which consists of only two arm techniques (*Gedan barai* and *Chudan oi-zuke*) and one stance (*Zenkutsu-dachi*). It consists of 24 movements and takes an expert less than 10 seconds to perform although a beginner might take about 40 seconds. The remaining five *Shotokan Heian* (Peaceful Mind) forms, cover almost all the basic techniques and stances. It is most important that these early *Kata* are properly learnt as bad habits can otherwise be acquired. In this sense they are much more important than the advanced *Kata*. For this, a good instructor is necessary. They cannot be effectively learnt from a book.

The more comprehensive and advanced *Katas* such as *Kanku* (*Kwanku* in Okinawan, or *Kushanku* in Chinese) incorporate quick changes of technique, slowness and quickness, maintenance of balance, stretching and bending of the body, correct breathing, body shifting combinations of hand and foot techniques and alternate tensing and relaxing of the muscles to facilitate the application and withdrawal of power. *Kanku* consists of 65 movements and takes some two minutes for even an expert to perform. It is therefore a memorised record of a whole range of techniques.

Since the 1950s competitions have also been held in *Kata*, with points being awarded by seven judges. A ten-point scoring system is normally used with the top and bottom score being deleted and the remainder being added together. This type of competition is particularly suitable for women as female *Jiu-kumite* is not generally considered desirable.

The emphasis placed upon *Kata* by the different styles varies. Virtually all styles consider it good for grooving the basic skills and it can also develop stamina and strength. Not all would agree as to its direct combat applicability. *Kyokushinkai* would consider that the latter requires actual combat training. *Shotokan, Shotokai, Wadoryu* and *Shukokai* might consider *Kata* to have a more direct applicability.

One of the great *Kata* exponents was Funakoshi Gichin, the man who introduced Karate to Japan and opened the Shotokan school which gave its name to a style. It is interesting to note that over half of his recently translated book, *Karate-do Kyohan*, relates to *Kata*. This shows the emphasis he placed upon it. For the student of *Kata* it is an invaluable publication. He classified *Kata* into two categories which stressed respectively power and strength or lightness and speed. In the power-strength group he placed among others the *Jutte* (Ten Hands,) *Hangetsu* (Half Moon), *Jion* (named after a Buddhist Saint), *Tekki* (Horse Riding) *Katas* and others. To watch a strong powerful man such as Keinosuki Enoeda (7th Dan, *Shotokan*) perform such a *Kata* is extremely impressive. In the speed category Funakoshi included *Heian* (Peaceful Mind), *Bassai* (To penetrate a fortress), *Kwanku* (named after its Chinese originator, Ku Shanku), *Empi* (Flying Swallow), *Gankaku* (Crane on a Rock) and others. These speed *Kata* tend to be the preserve of smaller men capable of rapid attack and retreat. One such expert is Tatsuo Suzuki (7th Dan, *Wadoryu*).

Before learning *Kata*, however, it is obviously necessary to have a basic grasp of the techniques involved. This means that the techniques have to be broken down into small units and practised separately. This was how *Kihon* (basic training) came to be devised. The individual techniques are later joined together to form a *Kata* and practised as a total unit.

Because of their great training value a good *karateka* will also perfect his *Kata* before concentrating on free fighting. To acquire control and exactness the beginner will perform his *Kata* relatively slowly. The expert will build up as much explosiveness and speed as possible and will completely lose himself in the

movement. To the onlooker it can look like a strangely impressive militant dance. *Kata* also provides the opportunity to create an opponent in the mind and to execute the movement totally, without any of the restrictions imposed in *Jiu-kumite* (Free fighting). It permits a vast range of techniques forbidden in competition or enables them to be executed in circumstances that competition would advise against, if not positively preclude. For example, a punch to the face of an opponent moving towards you is technically ideal, as both his and your movement combine to provide impact. Unless perfectly executed and controlled, however, under WUKO rules such a punch would risk disqualification. Even in *Kyokushinkai* 'knock-down' competition, punches to the face are not permitted. The technique can therefore only effectively be practised in *Kihon* and *Kata*. Of the two, *Kata* is the more realistic.

The practise of *Kata* also encourages analysis and control of movement. For example, two *Goju Kata* are the *Sanchin* and the *Tensho*. *Sanchin* stresses the 'Go' (hard), while *Tensho* stresses the 'Ju' (soft) elements of the style. The former is basically an isometric training exercise which develops deep muscular tension—

Above left: Shotokan
Above right: Wadoryu

as opposed to superficial facial grimaces. The legs are firmly tensed. Abdominal breathing is related to movement and the breathing-in action endeavours to push down the intestines. The effect is to strengthen the stomach, hip and leg positions. Mentally one may also think of making the muscles into steel. Immediately following tension, however, the muscles are at their most relaxed so *Ju* is also developed. In contrast the *Tensho Kata* stresses soft movements which nevertheless contain a deceptively strong, whip-like element. The two *Katas* therefore complement each other developing the opposing poles of softness and hardness which are quickly interchangeable. One might say that the *Goju* ideal is therefore to be like steel covered with cotton wool, with the opponent being unaware of which he is confronted with. In fact he is confronted with both simultaneously.

Some *Kata* are also performed very slowly rather like *Tai Chi*. This needs great control and concentration and enables exactness of movement to be attained. When thoroughly mastered, performance at a natural rate then presents no difficulty whatsoever. The concentration involved also provides training in self mastery and domination. With a genuine expert this atmosphere of control seems almost tangible and can be transformed into a psychological domination of potential opponents through the use of nothing more than the eyes. *Katas* can, incidentally, also be practised blindfold, thus developing positional sense and, indeed, almost a sixth sense concerning one's own and other movements in the immediate vicinity.

For the above reasons *Kata* training is vital to the full realisation of Karate potential. For those interested it is perhaps also the most straightforward of the Karate roads to the Zen world of nothingness. It would be most unfortunate if its current relative unpopularity with western *karateka* were to lead to the gradual demise of what is basically the essence of Karate.

For details concerning the individual *Kata* of specific styles the reader should refer to the books listed in Appendix B, or better still join an appropriate club.

8 Woodbreaking

Tamashiwari (Woodbreaking) is a subject about which there is a difference of opinion within Karate. All styles agree that *karateka* should be capable of such feats and that it is merely the natural outcome of techniques properly executed. Some styles, however, believe that its performance is merely flashy showmanship and whilst they may use it for the occasional public demonstration, it is rarely used within the *dojo*. Such showmanship may include breaking a stack of twenty roofing tiles, blocks of ice, bricks or large stones with the hand, elbow, foot or head. Other demonstrations include throwing a water melon into the air and thrusting the fingers through it as it descends or chopping the top off a bottle with the bare hand whilst leaving the bottle standing.

The style which particularly advocates *Tamashiwari* is *Kyokushinkai*. They claim that it is a physical and psychological necessity for *karateka* and that it even possesses a spiritual (Zen) significance. Their arguments include the following: The body's various striking points can be backed by quite remarkable power but this power can only be released when one has removed the fear of hitting something hard. Breaking is therefore a psychological as well as a physical ordeal, especially when performed in public. It requires great concentration and is as much, if not more, a mental as a physical effort. If one believes oneself capable of breaking the object then one can release one's entire physical energies into the act. Any mental reservations inhibit the maximum use of power. The word *Tamashi* in fact means 'trial' and *Tamashiwari* is therefore 'trial by wood'. Its successful execution gives self-confidence and 'self knowledge'. *Kyokushinkai* as well as *Tae Kwon do* (Korean Karate), requires their members to break specified thicknesses of wood before being permitted to take part in certain competitions or prior to being upgraded. This provides proof not only of power and that the joints can withstand impact, but also of the *karateka's* psychological commitment to the blow.

It is, of course, EXTREMELY DANGEROUS for an uncoached beginner to attempt *Tamashiwari*. Apart from the fact that the hands, etc., need a degree of conditioning, if the technique is improperly applied it can result in serious injury. It is also psychologically as well as physically dangerous as accidents can totally destroy self confidence. If, however, techniques are properly applied there need be no serious injury, other than possibly some bruising, even if the breaking attempt fails.

The other argument for *Tamashiwari* is rather esoteric and difficult for westerners to appreciate. It is claimed that the self discipline required is such that the strike is more a strike at oneself than at wood. The total commitment, concentration and absorbtion in the action is such that the *karateka's* ego can be temporarily obliterated, he transcends his normal nature and momentarily enters the Zen world of nothingness. In this context *Tamashiwari* can therefore provide 'Enlightenment through a single blow' in what amounts to active Zen meditation. Put rather more simply and in western non-Zen terms, for at least a few seconds the *karateka* is in a state of total involvement and identification with his environment and his action. Asked to describe this sensation a senior *karateka* once said, 'No, it's not like floating on a cloud. It's more like being totally alive or awake. It was just a feeling I didn't want to end. When I feel like that I'm invincible.'

At a more mundane level *Tamashiwari* also provides a personal, if apparently masochistic satisfaction and an obvious sense of achievement if one is operating at the limits of one's ability. Provided one accepts the limitations of age, whilst retaining enthusiasm, does not envy or endeavour to maintain the standards of one's youth, it can also continue to give some pleasure.

The author once received a letter from a young boy who wished to take up Karate. It read, 'I am six years old. Please tell me where I can join a Karate club. I am very keen and can break a pencil and six lollipop sticks. Can I become an international?' If an enthusiasm like that can be retained, anything is possible.

9 Competition

The most popular and exciting aspect of Karate is undoubtedly *Jiu-kumite*, or free-style sparring, which is always between two *Karateka* irrespective of grade. Originally fights were often to the death and such fights are known to have persisted in Hong Kong, for example, until declared illegal in the late 19th century. Apart from further organising the combat techniques of Karate, the Japanese also originated *Jiu-kumite* and by imposing combat rules, regulations and strict discipline enabled one aspect of Karate to be engaged in as a sport. Most Okinawan styles did not accept the sporting concept until the mid 1940s and some still do not.

Kumite attempts to provide the opportunity to combine most of what has been learned in reasonably realistic conditions. Some styles therefore consider it the natural culmination of all previous training. Because of the restrictions imposed on the techniques and the degree of contact permissible, some other styles consider it virtually a game of tag, lacking lethality and do not therefore take part. They believe that any *do* (way) aims at self-perfection and that modifications designed to popularise and make it into a sport remove it from its classical origin and destroy its nature. Karate might in fact be compared to an iceberg, only the sporting, *Kumite*, tip of which appears above the surface. Most Karate lies unseen beneath the water and is more in line with the original *budo* (fighting way) spirit.

Apart from those styles which do not indulge in competition, one of the distinguishing factors between different styles lie in their competition rules. *Kyokushinkai*, for example, permits extensive bodily contact and holds knock-down competitions, whilst others such as *Shukokai* emphasise non-contact. For this reason inter-style competition was for many years considered to be impossible and it was only after the formation of the Federation of All Japan Karate Organisations (FAJKO) in 1964, that a set of rules were devised which enabled inter-style and genuine world championships to be held. The rules adopted forbid the use of certain techniques such as spear or knife hand or *kin-geri* (kick to the groin) and are generally non-contact. They are for example, more similar to those of *Shukokai* than *Kyokushinkai*. It has in fact been claimed that *Shukokai* was devised specifically for sporting competition and it is certainly very successful competitively. Stressing, as it does, speed of movement and strong control the point-winning possibilities are high and the risk of disqualification low. To compete under FAJKO rules a *Kyokushinkai* man has to modify his style or almost certainly be disqualified. In many countries this is done. The main Japanese *Kyokushinkai* organisation however is not affiliated to FAJKO and regrettably does not take part in the all-style world championship. Through their 'knock-down' competitions they endeavour to stay nearer to the original *Budo* spirit and they tend to keep themselves to themselves.

When competitions are held they are controlled by a referee, who moves freely within the contest area, assisted by four judges posted at the corners. Outside the contest area there may also be a controller or senior official who the referee may consult if he wishes. Prime responsibility lies with the referee. Competition is normally in an area 8–10 metres square and lasts 2 or 3 minutes with time being allowed for stoppages. The scoring area consists of the front and back of the trunk and the entire head.

Before a contest the *karateka* perform a standing *rei* (bow) and the referee then calls '*Hajime*' (begin). All instructions are in Japanese. The waiting position is one of watchful, though relaxed, preparedness. Some *Karateka* specialise in counter-attack and rarely make the first move. In many respects *kumite* resembles boxing, except that attacks are stopped just short of contact. As the fists are ungloved, and as all parts of the body are used for striking, the reason for this is obvious. One of the tests of proficiency in Karate is, in fact, the ability to stop a fully focused attack just short of contact. Not to do so would result in disqualification.

The actual sparring consists of a free exchange of blows, blocks and counter-attacks until one player gets a fully focused blow to the target area. If the blow is delivered from a good stance, from the correct distance, is fully focused and spirited, an *ippon* (point) will be awarded and the contest is over. If the blow would be effective, but there is something incorrect about its delivery, a *waza-ari* (half-point) will be awarded. The fight will then continue until time is called, or one player obtains a full point or two half-points. If a team contest is being held, the teams consist of five individuals and the team with the greatest number of winning members is declared the winner.

As the judging of Karate contests involves subjective judgements by the officials, disputes over decisions have perhaps been unavoidable in the past. With wider knowledge of the rules among competitors and greater experience among officials this fortunately is on the decline. The introduction of video tapes may, however, be a useful aid to officials, and could amount to a fifth judge capable of instant replay. As referees invariably stop the contest in order to consult the judges in possible point-winning situations, the use of video tape would not interfere either with the natural rhythm of a Karate contest, or with the referee's ultimate responsibility.

Another possible improvement to competitions from a spectator's point of view might be the substitution of a three- for a one-point system. The one-point system gives a distinct advantage to the counter-puncher who is not normally the most interesting of fighters to watch. This change would lead to greater adventurousness in competition as one good counter-punch would not mean instant defeat. However, despite the one-point system, Karate contests have a great popular appeal and, at many of the major tournaments, hundreds of disappointed would-be spectators are regularly turned away at the door.

Training for competition

The first essential is to understand the rules of the competition under which one is proposing to compete. As mentioned previously these vary considerably from style to style and it certainly cannot be assumed that someone who is good at one style will automatically be good at another.

It is also advisable to do a lot of repetition work on one particular technique until it becomes perfect. This can be done in one-step, three-step and free-fighting practice. You should then work on a second and later a third technique whilst continuing also to practise the first. In this way, all three techniques become thoroughly 'grooved'. This is not to imply that other attacks should not also be learnt but a degree of specialisation and excellence is required for successful competition.

Attacks particularly suited to WUKO/FAJKO competition are *mae-geri* (front kick), *gyaku-zuki* (counter-punch with rear hand) and *oi-zuki* (lunge punch). To avoid possible disqualification it is wise not to use *gyaku-zuki* to the face of an opponent moving forward, but to concentrate on the body. Although *karateka* who rely entirely upon these techniques can be rather boring to watch it is unwise to attack with other techniques unless they have been thoroughly mastered. For example, the slightest mistake with *mawashi-geri* (roundhouse or circular kick with the rear foot) lays one open to *gyaku-zuki*.

All stances and techniques have their strengths and weaknesses. It is necessary to know these in order to avoid falling into inbuilt traps. For example, Billy Higgins, runner up in the 1972 World Individual Championships, tends to fight in a broad diagonal Horse or Straddle stance (*kiba-dachi*) which is vulnerable to leg sweeps (*de-ashi-barai*). However, being well aware of this potential weakness, he is able to adjust his stance rapidly. His awareness is such that he has himself become a master of leg sweeps.

Finally, I do not think it superfluous to add that one can only become a competent competitor through competitive experience. You should therefore endeavour to get as much of this as possible both in *dojo* training and actual competition.

Free-fighting tactics

'When the enemy advances, we retreat!
When the enemy halts, we harass!
When the enemy seeks to avoid battle, we attack!
When the enemy retreats, we pursue!'

Mao Tse-Tung

Opposite page: W. Higgins (GB) dominates his opponent (*Photo: The John Smith Press Agency*)

If possible one should watch future opponents in preliminary bouts and analyse their style, strengths and weaknesses. In team or big international tournaments this may not be possible for the individual *karateka* but it should be possible for the team manager or his assistants. The analysis can afterwards be passed to the fighter who then enters the arena with a degree of foreknowledge. It may also affect last-minute selection where substitution is allowable in team matches.

In the first half minute or so the fighter should probe his opponent in order to confirm the analysis. Feign a few attacks to ascertain his resources and possibly to confuse him. Locate his weak points for subsequent attack and his strong points so that they can be avoided. Break occasionally, adjust position and renew the probe. Try a few distracting hand movements to see if the opponent's eyes follow the moves. If they do, such movements might be used to create an opening for an attack. Ideally, of course, the eyes should encompass the whole situation without following any individual movements.

Do not move backwards in a straight line as it provides an obvious line of attack for the opponent. Move back and to right and left. If possible get some idea of the opponent's plans, if he has any. For example, if he attacks mainly with the right foot or fist, try rotating to his left. In this way you can suffocate and frustrate his plans which might agitate and destroy his morale. Also try to ascertain his timing and pattern of movement. You can then utilise these to attack when not expected.

A knowledge of those techniques which are possible or likely from individual stances is also helpful. For example, if the opponent persistently adopts the Forward stance (*Zenkutsu-dachi*), kicks with the front leg are most unlikely. On the other hand, if his rear foot position tends to point sideways, kicks with the rear leg are equally unlikely.

Endeavour to achieve psychological domination. In a boxing context Muhammad Ali was a master of this. Methods vary with circumstances but if the opponent *kiais* or shouts at you, you might shout back—louder. Let him know that you are not frightened and, if possible, frighten him. If you feel worried do not show it. Enter into the spirit of the contest and expect anything and everything. Edge slowly into striking distance and become as one with the opponent. Your own movement only has meaning in relation to his. If he attacks, become part of his movement as if in a synchronised dance. Do not merely stand back and move around independently as if a separate entity. 'Do not gobble proffered bait as the fish that covets bait gets caught.'

Try to ascertain the spirit or determination of your opponent.

Is it strong or weak? Is it aggressive or defensive? Does it lead or does it counter-punch? Look into his mind and become the opponent. Understand him and his reactions, but remember that not all people react alike. Look at him from outside as it were, not just from your own standpoint. Large and small men may psychologically and physically react totally differently to similar situations; so may people of different nationalities, or individuals trained by different coaches. Try to be sensitive to this. Here lies the benefit of experience and research. Do not let your own spirit show. In general, avoid retreat unless specifically intended to mislead, cause over confidence or create a counter-punching situation.

Think of the opponent as an enemy—an enemy to be defeated not just superficially but at his roots. Destroy his morale. In a team tournament this can be vital. Success breeds success. Defeat can lead to a feeling of hopelessness and inertia. Even if retreating, endeavour to control and predetermine your opponent's movements by presenting him with the alternatives you wish him to have. In short, try to lead him by the nose or act as a puppet master. When he attacks with spirit, stay calm. He may then relax and you can counter-attack. You may also influence his attitude by whether your own appears strong, weak, bored, worried, etc., and also by the hardness of your blocks. A hard *gedan-barai* may well make him think twice before trying another *mae-geri*.

The above approach should be adopted so that, as far as possible, it becomes automatic. Ideally, there should be no conscious thought at all, no worrying about the past or the future, the opponent, the crowd or other extraneous events. The man whose mind is distracted is bound to lose. Instead, be cocooned in a state of impassive concentration, totally involved in the here and now, responding to situations as they occur. When the opportunity appears 'attack like the wind' so that 'when the thunder clap comes the enemy has no time to cover his ears'. Do not, however, over commit yourself and if the attack fails move naturally into a further attack or retreat.

Be sensitive to changes in his spirit. Is it flourishing or waning? When it starts to collapse, pursue him and crush him. If you do not, he may recover. Make the most of your opportunities as they occur.

For a small man it is wise not only to come like the wind but also to go like lightning. To maintain a close fighting position with a bigger stronger opponent is foolhardy. In such circumstances one might withdraw and carefully set up the opponent for an attack or counter-attack. One might feign weakness or lack of spirit, move away, leave a selected attacking line open to the opponent, then block and counter-attack. Deception and surprise should be the keynote. In the words of the Japanese military strategist Kusonoki Masahige: 'When faced with a great enemy, practise deceit.' His favourite tactics were to harass, weary, confuse and mislead the enemy. Sound advice for the competitive *karateka*. This is also the philosophy of a guerrilla army faced with superior forces. Hence the above quotation from Mao Tse-Tung which is itself adopted from Sun Szu's *The Art of War*. However, if forced into a close defensive position, one should be 'calmly majestic as the forest and as steadfast as the mountains.' A panic reaction is fatal.

When you have executed a successful attack and possibly obtained a half-point, do not, in general, repeat the same manoeuvre. As stated previously, any technique has its weaknesses as well as strengths and, assuming that the opponent is capable of learning by his mistakes, repetition is dangerous.

To summarise: train to the point of instinctiveness, know your opponent and yourself, anticipate and suffocate his actions, destroy his morale, work for an opening and when the opportunity comes 'explode' and, if necessary, pursue, pursue.

10 Britain and the 1972 World Championships

In 1960 there were only a handful of *Karateka* in the whole of Britain. As the 1960s progressed recruits poured in and demand for instructors far exceeded supply. The money-earning potential was considerable and not surprisingly many self-qualified and self-appointed instructors emerged. Advertising was often of a low order particularly as rival associations were competing for the same market. Public concern grew, becoming particularly acute when in 1965 a notorious murder occurred in which it was claimed that Karate had been used. The judge recommended that a ban on Karate be considered and a Home Office inquiry followed. Although it was found that the vast majority of clubs were perfectly reputable, the main rival associations nevertheless agreed to form a federation designed to ensure an effective and controlled development of Karate. The British Karate Control Commission therefore came into being.

Within the BKCC, however, the separate associations retained their autonomy. Differences of opinion, techniques and ambitions differed and at times open disagreement flared—as for instance over whether or not to employ Japanese instructors. Dominant personalities within the associations clashed sometimes in print and the combative mentality of those drawn to Karate continued to demonstrate itself. At some meetings the casual spectator might well have been excused for thinking that he had arrived in error at a massed gladiatorial contest with all combatants subtly disguised as 20th-century committee men. Whatever else he might have felt, it certainly would not have been boredom. In such circumstances the mere survival of the BKCC speaks volumes for the basic common sense of the individuals concerned. Ultimately, even former deadly enemies acquired a somewhat amused affection for each other, allowed for each other's deficiencies and began to feel a genuine unity.

BKCC Executive Committee

The advent of recognition by the Sports Council assured the BKCC's future. Grant aid became available as did the use of the highly prized National Sports Centres, such as Crystal Palace, for the staging of Championships and courses for BKCC associations. Other Government Departments also asked the advice of the BKCC concerning applications for work permits by overseas Karate instructors, and many local authorities consulted them on the question of the use of public facilities for Karate classes and the appointment of properly qualified instructors. Gradually the advantages of BKCC membership became more and more apparent and all the major associations joined. With an increasingly co-operative and forward-looking Executive Committee the

BKCC strengthened its position as the first federal all-style organisation in the world.

Inter-style rivalry continued to be intense and the atmosphere at the annual all-style British Championships, to which each association brought an army of informed and vociferous supporters, was electric. Britain had hit upon a winning formula for international competition—intense rivalry between the separate styles leading to the creation of a select all-style squad and a highly-developed team spirit. It was this blending of technical and administrative strength at both association and BKCC level, drawing on the skills of a large number of people, both British and Japanese, that laid the basis for the enormous development of British Karate in the late 1960s and early 1970s. Accustomed to a very authoritarian approach in which the senior instructor's word is law, some Japanese instructors found it difficult to adapt to the democratic committee structure favoured by the West and attempted to control their organisations administratively as well as technically. Britain was fortunate in its personalities in that when problems occurred, as they inevitably did, a compromise based on mutual confidence was always found.

By the time of the Second World Championships the British squad, consisting of some thirty *karateka* from six associations, were in regular weekend training. The object of this training was not only to improve competition techniques and benefit by a cross fertilisation of styles but to build a team spirit. The loyalties of the individuals were first and foremost to their own styles and associations, but for the purpose of the Championship they had to be welded into a close-knit team. Cliques had to be broken and a new super clique formed. Room allocation was used specifically to achieve this end. A feeling of mutual trust had to be fostered between management and team so that each man knew what was expected of him, whether it be to fight, coach, film, arrange transport, hunt-out lost baggage, translate or ensure that meals were of the right sort and at the right time. Maximum use was therefore made of everyone prepared to help, so that in the Championships itself 'the brave could fight, the cautious defend and the wise counsel,' without distraction.

The training of a multi-style squad also presented technical difficulties as all members had to feel that they were benefiting. Furthermore, any competition operates to a certain set of rules and it does not follow that someone who would be a world champion at one style would be so at another or under the World Union All-style Competition Rules. The team therefore had to be selected with an eye specifically to the WUKO rules.

British World Championship
Team and officials 1972

When the final travelling squad of eleven fighters was selected such was the team spirit that even the disappointed nineteen gave the others a standing ovation. The team and supporters travelled to Paris in two chartered aircraft backed by a substantial physical and psychological build-up and accompanied by its own highly qualified doctor, who was himself an ex-wrestler and teacher of physical education. His mere presence gave the fighters confidence. The emotional drive to win was comparable to that of a holy war. Pressure was maintained right up to the end and the final team of five was only selected twenty-four hours before the tournament.

The preliminary rounds took place in two areas and apart from Team Manager Steve Arneil, who always remained with his team, there were a further three technical assistants who watched all competitions and noted the strengths and weaknesses of potential opponents. These were reported to Arneil who advised accordingly on tactics. During the tournament Arneil's advice and quick decisions were such that he was nicknamed 'the fox', if a somewhat noisy one, by the French press.

In the first round Britain defeated Trinidad and Tobago by 5 contests to nil and in the second round Canada by 3–1, with 1 draw. Meanwhile, Japan had defeated Holland, and France eliminated Brazil. Other winners in the same pool were Italy, Switzerland, U.S.A. and South Africa. Britain's opponents in the 3rd round were Japan, who had virtually the same team as had defeated them two years earlier in Tokyo. Few people gave much for Britain's chances.

In the first bout Stan Knighton fought Oishi who for three years had been National *Shotokan* Champion of Japan. Everyone waited to see how long Knighton would last—but instead he attacked, taking the fight to Oishi and scored a half-point with *Gyaku-zuki* and winning by judges' decision. This was a tremendous psychological boost to the British and a severe blow to the Japanese who had seen their champion defeated. In the next bout the British captain, Terry O'Neill, met Abe. For the entire bout Abe was forced to defend himself against a continuous barrage of round house, back and side kicks and was unable to launch any decisive attack. Two of the four judges gave the decision to O'Neill and the other two awarded a draw. When the referee awarded a draw the entire arena erupted in protest as O'Neill had clearly dominated the fight. Britain were unlucky not to be two matches ahead.

O'Neill (GB) attacks Abe (Japan) (*Photo: The John Smith Press Agency*)

In the third fight Glen Haslem, although he put in some good attacks was defeated by Iida, the first all-style Japanese champion. The team score was now equal. The fourth fight saw 5 ft. 8 in. Hamish Adam against the 6 ft. 2 in. Tabata who, although he had never won a major Japanese championship, had been runner up over a number of years. After a few near misses by Adam, Tabata decided that the match was not going to be as easy as his early contemptuous manner had implied. He mounted a sustained and fierce assault which Adam withstood. After continual contact Tabata was finally disqualified and Britain again led by 2 wins to 1 defeat with 1 draw.

Billy Higgins went into the final bout only having to draw for Britain to go through to the quarter finals. The atmosphere in the stadium was very hushed and tense as everyone realised they might be seeing history in the making. Higgins went out against Tanaka determined to win rather than draw. Tanaka, however, was equally determined and the result was a draw. Britain had defeated Japan.

Great Britain defeat Japan (Photo: The John Smith Press Agency)

For the next ten minutes the Coubertin stadium was a total shambles. Reporters ran out of the building as if Samson had just caused the roof to collapse. British supporters and officials, wet-eyed with jubilation danced and hugged each other. After this anything would be an anti-climax. Sportingly the Japanese officials marched up and congratulated the British team.

In the same round Italy defeated Switzerland, the U.S.A. beat South Africa and France eliminated Singapore.

In the fourth round Britain met Italy and, possibly somewhat over-confident, were beaten by the closest of possible margins—1–0 with four draws. Fortunately, they came back in the repêchage system, defeating Switzerland 3–1 with 1 draw in the fifth round. They now met France in the semi-final. France were traditionally the strongest Karate country in Europe, and fighting before their home supporters they would undoubtedly be hard to beat. Having reached a psychological peak against Japan, the British team may also have lost some of its edge. Led by their redoubtable captain

Dominique Valera the French won 3–0 with 2 draws and moved on to the final.

Meanwhile, Singapore returned through the repêchage to meet the U.S.A. Possibly over anxious and eager to equal or even improve on their position in the 1970 World Championships, several members of the American team were warned or disqualified for making contact and they thereupon withdrew from the tournament. Unfortunately, due to injuries Singapore were also unable to move on and meet Italy in the second semi-final. In the final France, again spurred on by home support, defeated Italy 3–1 with 1 draw to become the new World Champions.

The following day in the individual championship, in which there were over a hundred entries, Britain again had considerable success. Higgins won the silver medal being defeated in the final by Watanabe, a Brazilian naturalised Japanese. Donovan and Wade, two other Britons, were also in the first eight.

Although obviously pleased with their performance the British team were undoubtedly disappointed at having beaten Japan and then to have let the world crown slip through their fingers. Despite the consoling and generous remarks of Monsieur Delcourt, Chairman of the French Karate Union, and newly appointed Chairman of the World Union, that 'France are World Champions but Britain have made history,' this last minute failure undoubtedly rankled. It was nearly a year before Britain had their chance of revenge.

In January 1973 Britain joined the European Economic Community (Common Market) and to celebrate the occasion a number of cultural and sporting events were held with the support of the Government 'Fanfare for Europe' Committee. One such event was a France versus Great Britain Karate match at the Crystal Palace National Sports Centre. Such was the drawing power of these two teams that all seats were sold weeks beforehand. For fear of attracting unmanageable crowds the BKCC publicly advertised that no further tickets were available. Despite this, hundreds of spectators had to be turned away.

The British preparation had again been very systematic. Each team consisted of 10 *karateka* and 2 reserves. At the mid-point in the tournament France led 4–1 with 5 draws. It looked as if the World Champions would continue to be undefeated. However, Britain stormed back in the second half, not conceding one bout, eventually winning by 6–4 (with 10 draws). They thus confirmed their position as one of the world's top Karate countries, alongside France and Japan.

Appropriately, soon afterwards various Karate political problems were also overcome and Britain joined the European Karate Union. It seemed that some semblance of international unity was coming to Karate—at least so far as Europe was concerned.

11 The Organisation of World and British Karate

The structure of World Karate is exceedingly complex due to the multitude of styles each with its own national and international organisation. Particularly outside of Japan these associations have tended to dispute each other's credentials and the general situation has been one more of chaos than organisation. When the Federation of All Japan Karatedo Organisations (FAJKO) was formed in 1964, the beginnings of a world structure began to emerge, although, regrettably, not all Japanese associations joined. By 1970 with the formation of the World Union of Karatedo Organisations (WUKO) a semblance of order had arrived.

Separate countries tackled their own individual chaos in different ways. France created a central all-style organisation with strong Government backing and the minor single-style associations gradually died away. Britain, on the other hand, permitted the separate single-style associations to continue to exist but formed a federal, umbrella organisation, the BKCC, to which all major associations affiliated. Some other countries adopted patterns similar to France, while Britain have also received many requests for advice concerning the formation of federal organisations. Yet other countries remain in a state of internal anarchy with as many as a dozen groups purporting to be the official body and an equivalent number of supposedly international teams claiming representation.

In view of the considerable interest expressed in the BKCC structure some general information about it is given below. Membership provides associations with the following services:

(a) Direct financial assistance to associations to help them stage their own coaching courses and enable them to send teams to take part in international single-style competitions overseas.
(b) Selected *karateka* can attend BKCC-financed squad training sessions, referees' courses and be selected for full international teams.

(c) Numerous administrative services such as:

Preparation and publication of competition rules and other documents.
Assistance with staging championships and publicity.
Travel agency services.
Clearing house services for applications to join clubs.

(d) Access to National Sports Centres. Applications for the use of these centres must be submitted via the BKCC, so non-affiliated clubs do not normally have access.

(e) Assistance in obtaining permanent or temporary work permits for overseas instructors which the association wish to employ.

(f) Assistance with applications by individuals to instruct in evening institutes and in gaining access to local authority controlled premises. Many local authorities only permit their facilities to be used by BKCC-approved clubs and instructors.

In addition to affiliating to the BKCC, individual associations normally also affiliate to the Japanese-based Headquarters of their own specific style. In most instances that Headquarters affiliates to FAJKO, the Japanese equivalent of the BKCC. The BKCC also affiliates to the all-style European Karate Union (EUK), as do other countries, although their membership of WUKO is independent of their representation on the European organisation. British associations are also likely to be affiliated to the European Headquarters for their own style. The effect of this complicated structure is that it is possible to take part in both single-style and all-style championships at national, international, European and World level. The address of the British Karate Control Commission and its member associations as in 1974 are as follows:

Key	Name	Style	Secretary
BKCC	British Karate Control Commission	All-style Federation	B. Williams, 4/16 Deptford Bridge London, SE8 4JS
BKG	British Karate Gojukai	*Gojukai*	S. Morris, London Gojukai, 9 Earlham Street, London, WC2
BKA	British Karate Association	No specific style	L. Palmer, 77 Cambridge Road, W. Wimbledon, London, SW20

Key	Name	Style	Secretary
BKF	British Karate Federation	*Yoseikan*	E. Brentnall, 96 Hampden Road, Chingford, London, E.4.
BKK	British Karate Kyokushinkai	*Kyokushinkai*	K. Morris, 8 Southwood Ave., Kingston upon Thames, Surrey
KDS	Karatedo Shotokai	*Shotokai*	J. Wood, 52 Framfield Road, Hanwell, London, W.7.
KUGB	Karate Union of Great Britain	*Shotokan*	C. Hepburn, 5 Darley Road, Manchester, M16 0DG
SKU	Shukokai Karate Union	*Shukokai*	A. Woodhouse, 44 Gleadless Common, Sheffield, 12
UKKF	United Kingdom Karate Federation	*Wadoryu*	J. Green, 10 Brackley, Queens Road, Weybridge, Surrey
SKBC	Scottish Karate Board of Control	All style federation	A. McGregor, 5 Stoneywood Park, Stoneywood, Denny, Stirlingshire

(This organisation is comparable to a BKCC for Scotland although it affiliates to the BKCC. Scotland and England enter separate teams in all-style European championships (EUK) but combine to form a British team for the World Championships.)

Key	Name	Style	Secretary
WKBC	Welsh Karate Board of Control	All style federation	H. Collins, 44 Albert Street, Miskin, Mountain Ash, Glamorgan

All the organisations representing the major Oriental martial arts practised in Britain (i.e. Karate, *Aikido*, *Tae-Kwan-do*, *Kendo*, *Kung Fu*, etc.), are also considering forming a martial arts federation. Should it be formed this federation is likely to be called the British Union of Martial Arts (BUMA).

The organisational pattern in Japan and their links with British and world associations is shown in the accompanying diagram. WUKO is the international controlling body with membership direct from individual countries. Countries may also affiliate to a continental all-style union where one exists. Continental all-style championships are normally held annually and World all-style championships at two or three yearly intervals. At present such unions exist for Europe (UEK), the Central American and Caribbean countries (CACKU) and the Asian and Pacific countries (APUKO).

Addresses of the major Japanese associations are as follows:

Key Japan	Name	Style	Secretary
WUKO	World Union of Karatedo Organisations	All style	WUKO Headquarters, Senpaku Shinko Building, 6th Floor, 35 Shiba-Kotohira-cho, Minato-ku, Tokyo, Japan
FAJKO	Federation of All Japan Karatedo Organisations	All style Federation	Address as WUKO
AJKF	All Japan Karate Federation	*Wadoryu*	2-1-16 Shimo-Ochiai, Shinjyuku-Ku, Tokyo, Japan
JKA	Japan Karate Association	*Shotokan*	3-1 Chome, Kouraku, Bunkyo-Ku, Tokyo
IKK	International Karate Kyokushinkai HQ	*Kyokushinkai*	M. Oyama, 3-9, 3-chome, Nishi-Ikebukuro, Toshima-ku, Tokyo
SWKU	Shukokai World Karate Union	*Shukokai*	7,8 Chome, Daikaidori, Hyogu-Ku, Kobe, Japan
GKF	Gojukai Karate Federation	*Gojukai*	Japan Karatedo College, 6-2 1-Chome, Zempukuji, Suginami-Ku, Tokyo

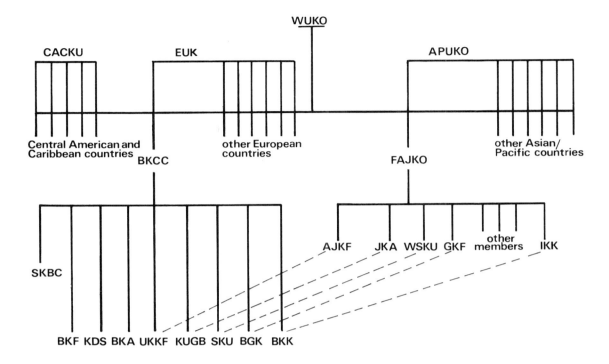

12 Origins and Distinctive Features of the Individual Styles

Gojuryu

Founded by Chojun Miyagi (1888–1953), an Okinawan who lived in China for many years where he studied Chinese *Kenpo*. Miyagi, a specialist in in–fighting, blended the soft Chinese movements with the hard Okinawan movements to form the *Goju* (Hard–Soft) school of Karate. This 'Hard–Soft' principle is a Karate application of the Chinese concept of *Yin* and *Yang* by which everything is understood to consist of combinations of opposites (female/male, hard/soft, good/bad, dark/light, etc.) i.e. without 'hard', 'soft' would have no meaning. *Goju* stresses a whole range of opposites of which hard and soft are only one example. Fast/slow and relaxation/tension are two other elements which emerge strongly in *Goju Kata*. When attacked fiercely (i.e. with *Go*) one defends with *Ju* and vice versa. By a change of tension *Ju* can also quickly become *Go*. This contrasts with *Shotokan*, for example, where there are many attacking blocks to counter hard attacks. *Goju* uses soft two-part counters and emphasises 'covering the cover'. It also emphasises mental attitude and its *Katas* tend to stress feeling and slow movement.

Many *Goju* postures are based upon the fighting postures of animals. *Goju* is a very strong style generally requiring good body development. On Miyagi's death Gogen Yamaguchi, nicknamed 'the Cat', because of his long hair and cat-like movements, became the senior *Goju* instructor. Yamaguchi recommends the practice of Yoga in conjunction with Karate, particularly for its strong breathing techniques and relaxation exercises. *Goju* probably places more emphasis on breathing than other styles. Miyagi used to practise the *Sanchin Kata* facing a fierce wind and emitting a roar like a lion.

Kyokushinkai

Founded by Masutatsu Oyama, born 1923 in Korea but resident in Japan since 1938. *Kyokushinkai* means 'The Peak of Truth'. Oyama lived a solitary life for two years in the mountains to strengthen his self-discipline. He was strongly influenced by Chinese techniques, and stresses *budo* Karate as opposed to 'sport' Karate. At one time or another he has, unarmed, fought 52 bulls. *Kyokushinkai* competitions can involve substantial body contact and 'knock-down' competitions are sometimes held in which kicks to the body and head are permitted and punches to the body but not to the head. Masks and padded jackets are also sometimes used in training to enable full contact to be made without injury. In many countries, but not Japan, *Kyokushinkai* also adapt their techniques to take part in all-style competitions.

There is considerable stress on *Tamashiwari* and before being promoted to a more senior grade the student must prove his ability to break a specified thickness of wood. In general this style is suited to those who like a robust approach to training and competition.

Shotokan

The word *Shotokan* originally meant 'Shoto's house' or 'hall'— 'Shoto' being the pen name of Funakoshi Gichin (1870–1957), the first Okinawan to bring *Tang hand* to Japan and, having incorporated certain elements of *Ju-Jitsu*, to rename it Karate. *Shotokan* was therefore the name given to Funakoshi's *dojo* which was opened in 1936. Following a split within his group in 1956, the words *Shotokan* and *Shotokai* were used to distinguish the two factions. The words have subsequently become associated with separate styles although, as the original split was not over a technical matter, some would claim that the degree of technical difference was not great.

Funakoshi was also a great originator and exponent of *Kata*, and *Shotokan* place great stress upon this. Unlike *Shotokai* they also take part in competition although this is not their only consideration. Since 1955 the chief instructor of the modern, professionally organised and internationally widespread *Shotokan* organisation, the Japan Karate Association (JKA), has been Masotashi Nakayama (born 1913). The JKA senior instructor for Europe is Keinosuke Enoeda (7th *Dan*) one of the technical advisers for this book.

Although when in competition, *Shotokan karateka* may move about lightly with a relatively high centre of gravity, in the act of punching they invariably adopt a low, strong stance with a wide foot position. This is to provide stability and enable maximum use of the leg and hip in creating power. This results in stances which tend to be diagonal to the opponent.

Shotokai

Shotokai means 'Shoto's Council' or 'Association'. Following a disagreement over a professional versus amateur approach to the teaching of Karate, the amateur advocates broke away from the JKA in 1956—they deplored what they considered to be the increasing popularisation and commercialisation of Karate. They took the name of *Shotokai* but consider themselves to be technically similar to *Shotokan*, although some differences have developed with the years.

Shotokai place considerable emphasis on the need for suppleness and they also use *Za Zen* (Sitting Meditation) more than most styles. They tend to use the one- or two-knuckle fist, rather than the forefist, for punching. The aim is to use the single knuckle rather like a stabbing spear. They do not practise *Tamashiwari* and, unlike *Shotokan*, do not take part in competition. As the object of Karate is to strike and as, with the exception of *Kyokushinkai*, this is prevented in competition, they consider Karate and competition to be incompatible.

Like *Shotokan*, in order to develop form, they place great emphasis upon *Kata*. They are, however, less strict about its precise interpretation, believing that, if it works for the individual concerned, that is all that is required. They believe this approach to be more pragmatic and less theoretic than *Shotokan*. The Senior *Shotokai* instructor for Europe is Mitsusuke Harada (5th *Dan*), one of the technical advisers for this book.

Shukokai

Founded by Chojiro Tani (born 1915). Tani first studied *Shitoryu* under Kenwa Mabuni, founder of that style. Broke away in 1950 to found *Shukokai* (Way for All). This is a speed style well suited to sport Karate under World Union (WUKO) rules. It stresses strong control and unlike, for example, *Kyokushinkai* contact in competition would receive immediate disqualification. Stances are designed more for mobility than stability and are not so low or broad-based as *Shotokan*. Hip positions are also squarer to the opponent. As the rear leg cannot be used to the same extent as in *Shotokan* to generate power, fast whip-like movements of the hips are used for this purpose.

Wadoryu

Founded by Hironori Otsuka (born 1892). He studied many different forms of *Ju-Jitsu* at Waseda University before founding the *Wadoryu* (Way of Peace) school of Karate. Otsuka has been Chairman of the Federation of All Japan Karatedo Organisations formed in 1964 and which embraces most Japanese-style organisations. The senior *Wado* instructor for Europe is Tatsuo Suzuki (7th *Dan*) one of the technical advisers for this book.

Wado is basically a speed style and, like *Shukokai*, well suited to World Union competitions. As regards stance, hip position and hip technique, it lies between *Shukokai* and *Shotokan*. This enables the rear leg to be used to some extent in generating power, whilst not sacrificing speed. It also places strong emphasis upon *Kata* training.

Shitoryu

Founded by Kenwa Mabuni, an Okinawan who studied under two separate instructors: Itosu and Higaonna. He blended their styles to form *Shitoryu*. The name was chosen to incorporate Japanese characters from the names of his two instructors. This is a speed style from which *Shukokai* is derived. Although a style with a large following in Japan, at the time of writing it is not practised in Britain.

13 Technical Advisers

Keinosuke Enoeda (7th *Dan*)—*Shotokan*
Born 1935 in Kyushu. Started practising Karate at the age of 15.
Studied *Shotokan* under Funakoshi and Nakayama. Also studied
Commerce at Takushoku University. In 1963 became JKA All-
Japan Champion and *Shotokan* Open International Champion.
Awarded 7th *Dan* in 1973. Chief Instructor to the All-European
Karate Federation (*Shotokan*) and the Karate Union of Great
Britain.

Tatsuo Suzuki (7th *Dan*)—*Wadoryu*
Born 1928 in Yokohama. Became interested in Karate at the age
of 14 and studied under H. Otsuka. In 1952 also obtained a degree
in Economics at Nihan Univesrity. In 1965 he was awarded the
7th *Dan*, highest Grade of the *Zen Nippon Karatedo Renmei*. Came
to Europe in 1965. He is now the Senior *Wado* Instructor in
Europe and Britain.

Mitsusuke Harada (5th *Dan*)—*Shotokai*
Born 1928 in Manchuria. Started studying Karate in 1943 under
Funakoshi in the *Shotokan dojo*. Received a 5th *Dan* direct from
Funakoshi. Also studied Economics and Commerce at Waseda
University. Went to work at a Japanese bank in Brazil and sub-
sequently became a professional Karate instructor. Came to
Britain in 1963 and is now Chief Instructor to the *Karate do
Shotokai.*

Steve Morris (6th *Dan*)—*Gojuryu*
Born 1942 in Wales. Interested in Martial Arts from an early age.
Wished to study under Yamaguchi and travelled to Japan for that
purpose. Also trained in *Kendo* and other weapons associated with
the martial arts. Senior British *Goju* instructor.

Steve Arneil (6th *Dan*)—*Kyokushinkai*
Born 1935 in South Africa. Studied *Kyokushinkai* for $4\frac{1}{2}$ years under M. Oyama in Japan. Is also 1st *Dan* Judo. First European in Japan to take on 100 fights consecutively lasting a total of $2\frac{3}{4}$ hours. Personal Karate tutor to the Jordanian Royal Family. Senior *Kyokushinkai* instructor in Britain. Coach to the British team since 1969, including the 1970 and 1972 World Championships.

Roy Stanhope (4th *Dan*)—*Shukokai*
Born 1945 in England. Studied Karate since 1962. Has practised *Wado* and *Shotokan* and obtained 1st *Dan* in each. Obtained 4th *Dan* in *Shukokai*. Member of the British team in the late 60s. Senior instructor to *Shukokai* Karate Union of Great Britain and Assistant Chief Instructor for European *Shukokai*.

14 How to Join the Best Karate Club

Most people joining a Karate club for the first time have little, if any, idea of what they want or what is available. They generally take what they are given and are not in a position to ask informed questions. They have some vague idea as to what they understand Karate to be but they are probably unaware of the existence of different styles and almost certainly unaware of what the differences consist of. Before joining any club it is therefore wise to shop around and to find out what constitutes the 'best buy'. What is appropriate for one person is not necessarily so for another. The following are some of the points which should be borne in mind:

1. Availability of clubs in the area

If your locality has only one club you have very little choice. Most towns, however, have several clubs often of different styles, so a choice should be possible. If in doubt check addresses with the nationally recognised Governing Body and then pay an investigatory visit to the clubs concerned.

2. Which style suits your physical and psychological characteristics?

People wanting heavy robust contact with some stress upon woodbreaking, etc., might like *Kyokushinkai*; whilst those wishing to exploit speed rather than power might prefer *Shukokai* or *Wadoryu*. The *Shotokan* style is in an intermediate position, possibly leaning towards a power emphasis. *Shukokai* was also devised specifically for competition under WUKO rules. It might therefore appeal to those hoping to achieve a high standard in international competitive sporting Karate. Further details concerning differences between styles are given in Chapter 12. There are also some clubs which are styleless or purport to practise all styles. The latter is not really feasible and you should press to know which style they lean towards.

A first-class natural athlete will, of course, excel in whichever style he chooses but even so there is likely to be a style particularly suited to his characteristics. It is also advisable, at least in the first instance, to confine oneself to one style. It is not practical to learn them all well. At an advanced stage an examination of other styles is useful, but even then it is wise not to try and do too much. The essence of a good *Karateka* is instinctive reaction and diversification can weaken this.

3. Is there a probability of your moving to another part of the country?

If so, it is advisable to join a style which has clubs on a national basis. To move and then to have to change styles can be very frustrating. Apart from having to re-learn one's techniques it may also mean that hard-earned grading qualifications may not be recognised. Different styles predominate in different countries and different parts of countries so enquiries may need to be made with the main national association.

4. Does the club possess a good instructor?

A good instructor is vital to effective progress. It may, however, sometimes be necessary to check that the instructor's qualifications are what he claims them to be as it is not unknown for some to award themselves fictitious *Dan* grades. These qualifications can normally be checked with the nationally recognised Governing Body. If possible, try to see the instructor teaching a class before you finally join. Tastes vary and what is a good instructor for one person may not be so for another. Some like a hard working, strongly physical, approach while others prefer a technical analytical attitude.

5. Is the club a member of the nationally recognised organisation?

If not, grades awarded would not be recognised elsewhere and in Britain, for example, the club would receive none of the benefits noted in Chapter 11. It would probably also be quite impossible for those even with the ability to achieve full international status.

6. Cost of instruction

Fees vary from club to club, from association to association and from one country to another. In Britain in early 1974 the average fees were roughly as follows:

Junior:	50p per hour
Adults:	75p per hour
Association licence:	£4 per annum
Clothing:	£10

Private instruction is also possible but fees would need to be negotiated beforehand with the instructor concerned.

7. Quality of the dojo and its equipment
This is significant although not as vital as a really good instructor. Without adequate space and training equipment, however, progress will inevitably be hampered.

8. Instruction by correspondence course
This is far inferior to joining a club and should be avoided if at all possible.

In order to obtain the best advice about clubs in Britain contact the BKCC. Alternatively, enquiries might be referred to the National or Regional Sports Council, a Citizen's Advice Bureau or a Local Authority Information Office.

15 Karate Injuries

By Mr. Peter R. Jordan, M.B., B.S., F.R.C.S. (Eng.), (*Medical Officer to the BKCC*)

Just as all activities in life produce their own pattern of illness, different sports inevitably produce their own pattern of injuries. Karate is no exception to this.

It would be easy to say, after the principles of competitive karate have been understood, that no injuries should be sustained if those principles are strictly applied. In practice this is unfortunately not the case, although it may come as a surprise to the uninitiated how relatively few injuries are incurred and that these are in the main trivial. This is particularly so at the highest level of competition.

During the last few years I have attended many competitive events in Great Britain and Europe—the level ranging from inter-club competition to international and world championship standard. When a statistical analysis is applied to the various types of injury and charted against the grade of competitor, it shows an inverse ratio of both incidence and severity of injury to the competitor's seniority.

Having made the above comments, I might add, as some solace to the novice (lest he feels entirely at fault by his own ineptness and may be discouraged from entering the competitive field), that in those different levels of competition other factors are also relevant; principally in those of adjudication. Of course it is an inescapable fact that the higher the level of competition the better is, or should be, the judging and refereeing.

Having mentioned how injuries are in general related to competition level, let us look at the types of injury that occur. These may be divided up into anatomical regions. In order of frequency they are: 1. Injuries to the face and neck; 2. Hands; 3. Feet.

Facial and neck injuries are fortunately, in the main, minor, but may, nevertheless, result in the termination of a contest. This is because evidence of contact is most obvious when facial injury is incurred. (The drawing of blood often results in the disqualification of the perpetrator!) The injuries most often encountered are:

Lacerations—usually around the lips and eyes, where a relatively thin layer of soft tissue overrides sharp ridges, i.e. the teeth and eyebrows. For example, in a recent international tournament, of the 16 injuries encountered, 7 were facial lacerations, 3 of which required to be sutured (stitched).

Contusions and abrasions constitute the bulk of the other injuries. Most are not serious in themselves, but can be most painful and sufficient to prevent a competitor from continuing in a contest or troublesome enough to interfere with training. Soft tissue injuries of this type are notoriously slow to resolve.

Bony and dental injuries, though rarer, are much more serious. The following injuries have occurred in tournaments and many warranted hospital admission and treatment:

Nasal fractures with depression or deviation of the bony bridge are relatively common. These injuries, though not particularly dangerous, can lead to later complications, such as obstructed nasal airways, intermittent nasal sinus blockage which may produce infection and chronic or recurrent sinusitis. It is for these reasons that I feel that a nasal fracture should be corrected early. This of course must be done in hospital with a suitable anaesthetic and the above comments, I hope, make it obvious that such treatment is not recommended simply to effect a cosmetic result! (though of course this must be taken into account).

Malar fractures. The cheeks are supported by an arch of bones constituting the zygomatic arch, under which part of the lower jaw moves and which is also related to the bony structures comprising the eye socket. A heavy blow to the malar (cheek) region quite readily produces a fracture of the zygomatic arch. This injury, in competitions I have witnessed, is fortunately rare. It is indeed often quite a difficult injury to diagnose even with the help of X-rays. Some of the effects it can produce are double vision, difficulty in opening the mouth and chewing, numbness of the cheek and inside the mouth, together with an ugly depression of the facial profile after the facial swelling has subsided. These results may well be permanent if the depressed bone is not re-aligned properly. This is again an operative procedure which needs to be done under anaesthesia in hospital. It is usually fairly easy to rectify if recognised and treated early but, if neglected and mal-union of the bones occurs, it is a most troublesome condition.

Dental and mandibular fractures are fairly frequent injuries, though often the degree of injury to this region is not very severe.

Loosened teeth, without fracture of the teeth themselves or underlying alveolar bone, is a common injury. Provided the teeth are sound, re-aligned and splinted soon after the injury, they will not be lost. Even teeth which are detached from their sockets, if quickly and accurately replaced, will usually become firm and survive. Never let an unqualified person pull out or discard loosened teeth. Artificial replacements are both costly and never so good as the original!

Mandibular fractures, i.e. fractures of the body of the lower jaw, are fortunately quite uncommon. They should always be regarded as serious. If they are unstable or badly displaced they will require operative correction and fixation. This is frequently done by wiring the upper and lower teeth together for six weeks. (The subsequent enforced liquid diet is not the ideal fare for athletes!)

Injuries to hands and feet are very common. *Both acute and chronic* soft tissue bruising occur in the contact areas, especially around the Metacarpo-phalangeal (knuckle) joint of the middle finger. In this region joint enlargement occurs after repeated bruising due to swelling of the soft tissues around the joint and synovial effusion into the joint. If the skin over the joint is broken, infection of the joint can occur. If this joint becomes especially tender or reddened following injury, a doctor should be consulted, for infection in the joint often results in permanent damage if left untreated.

Interphalangeal dislocations of fingers and toes are quite common. They occur usually after the digit has been twisted in a fold of clothing or following an awkward fall. Occasionally they can be reduced without anaesthetic by a doctor who is used to dealing with them, but normally an anaesthetic is necessary. Do not ever let an enthusiastic amateur try to 'put a dislocation back'. Pain and further damage to the joint is the usual outcome.

Fractures of the metacarpals (in the hand) *and metatarsals* (in the feet) are among the commoner injuries encountered. In competitions the index and middle metacarpals are the most frequently fractured; whereas in breaking techniques the little and ring finger metacarpals are those most often fractured. The metatarsals are less often fractured, and I have not noted any special pattern to this region.

These fractures should always be treated seriously. X-ray assessment to determine the type of fracture (spiral, angulated or comminuted). Accurate reduction and splintage are usually required to restore the configuration of the damaged hand or foot.

Dislocated shoulders have occurred in several competitions. Early reduction is always necessary and should be done by a doctor (although often the 'recurrent dislocator' has learned the trick of putting his own shoulder back!).

Conclusion. It is apparent then that Karate is not without its hazards, but compared with many supposed 'gentler' sports the injuries per competition are fewer and less severe.

Precautions. I would advocate all those engaged in competition and rigorous training to observe the following points to minimise the risk of injury.

(a) Keep finger and toenails well trimmed.

(b) Always wear a sound protective genital guard or box.

(c) Avoid using bandages and/or shinguards as these encourage more contact than is necessary and may mask or aggravate other injuries.

(d) Ensure that competitions have adequate medical attendance, either in the form of a doctor, nurse or competent first-aid team (the Red Cross or St. John's Ambulance Brigade are excellent voluntary bodies which will always attend if given sufficient warning).

(e) Never neglect injuries. Always seek medical advice at an early stage.

Appendices

List of Commonly Used Japanese Karate Terms

Ai-uchi : Simultaneous scoring with no points given
Chui : Warning
Dan : Degree
Deshi : Disciple, trainee
Dojo : Gymnasium
Encho : Prolonging the time of the match
Hajime : Start
Hansoku : Disqualification, foul
Hantei : Decision
Hikewake : Drawn result
Ippon : One, or one point
Karate gi : Karate kit

Karateka : One who practises Karate
Kata : Fixed sequence of techniques used for practising form
Kiai : Method of shouting, peculiar to Japanese martial arts
Kihon : Basic training
Kihon kumitei : Basic prearranged sparring
Kime : Focusing concentration and power
Kumitei : Sparring
Jiu-kumite : Free sparring
Kyu : Step in grading system
Kyukei : Rest
Magattei : Turn around, or about face
Makiwara : Punching board

Sambon kumitei : Form of basic sparring using three successive attacks
Sensei : Instructor
Shimpan : Referee, umpire, judge
Shobu : Match
Tsuzukete : Carry on, continue
Waza-ari : Half-point
Yame : Score made, or stop
Yoi : Get ready

Positions
Jodan : High
Chudan : Middle
Gedan : Low
Soto : Outer
Uchi : Inner
Hidari : Left
Migi : Right

APPENDIX B

Reference Books: by style

GOJURYU
Fundamentals of Gojuryu Karate by G. Yamaguchi (O'Hara Publications).
KYOKUSHINKAI
What is Karate by M. Oyama (Ward Lock & Co. Ltd.).
This is Karate by M. Oyama (Japan Publications Trading Co.).
Vital Karate by M. Oyama (Ward Lock & Co. Ltd.).
Modern Karate by S. Arneil and B. Dowler (Kaye & Ward Ltd.).
SHOTOKAN
Karate-do Kyohan by Gichin Funakoshi (Kodansha International Ltd.).
Dynamic Karate by M. Nakayama (Ward Lock & Co. Ltd.).
Karate by H. Nishiyama & R. C. Brown (Charles E. Tuttle & Co.).
WADORYU
Karate-do by T. Suzuki (Pelham Books Ltd.).